Copyright © 2018 by Debbie McNair-Allen
League City, Texas

All rights reserved under the Pan-American and International Copyright conventions

Printed in the United States of America

ISBN:978-0-9968711-4-3

All rights reserved. This book may not be reproduced in whole or part, in any form or by any means, electronic or mechanical, including photocopying, recording, or by any information storage and retrieval system now known or hereafter invented, without the permission of the author.

Unless otherwise indicated, Scriptures are taken from the King James Version. Copyright© 1979, 1980, 1982, Thomas Nelson, Inc., Publishers

Draped in Praise Publishing, LLC

Draped in Praise
P O Box 3231
League City, TX 77574
www.drapedinpraise.org

To God be the Glory…other books published by D.I.P.

The Woman at the Well: From Guilt to Grace
Across the Tracks by Dr. Dennis Brooks
Free to Be Me by Dr. Regina Biggurs-Ray
Live Free by Dianne Gradington
A Church Named Ruth by Dr. Dennis Brooks

Coming soon:
Spiritual H2O: Help to Overcome
Men Are Victims, Too!

Damaged Goods...

From

Shattered Pieces

To

Sacred Peace

The shame, the guilt, the rejection can lead to

discouragement, depression, and dysfunction....

Damaged Goods...
From Shattered Pieces to Sacred Peace

Preface

Introduction

1. Predestined for greatness

2. How the damage occurred

3. Shattered pieces leads to unfulfillment

4. Along the journey

5. Your past is not your destiny

6. Embracing the impossible

7. Get Pass Your Past

8. Restored versus refurbished

9. Sacred peace found in God

About the Author

"Be broken [in pieces], O peoples, and be shattered! Listen, all you [our enemies from the] far countries. Prepare yourselves [for war], and be shattered; Prepare yourselves [for war], and be shattered."

Isaiah 8:9 AMP

"He healeth the broken in heart, and bindeth up their wounds.

Psalms 147:3 KJV

Faithful are the wounds of a friend, But the kisses of an enemy are deceitful.

Proverbs 27:6 NKJV

Kind words heal and help; cutting words wound and maim.

Proverbs 15:4

Preface

Damaged Goods: From Shattered Pieces to Sacred Peace

is about the damaged emotions, mental, spiritual, financial, as well as physical damage that can occur from abuse and assault, which includes rejection that occurs in life. I may never know what it will feel like to celebrate 50 years of marriage. But I can say that I know how to love and what love is. I never regret giving my all to love unconditionally and as if I had never been hurt. There comes a time/season when one must stop allowing the same patterns to occur in life and trust God completely for His will.

These are experiences that led to my brokenness. I pray that you will understand how to recognize the things that can lead to brokenness. If you are already broken, my prayer is that you can find comfort and healing that will eventually lead to wholeness. There is hope for those who have been exposed, experienced, and survived domestic violence and all areas of abuse, as well as rejection. The word of God says in Jeremiah 29:11, "For I know the thoughts that I think toward you, saith the Lord, thoughts of peace, and not of evil to give you an expected end."

As a survivor of domestic violence and sexual assault, I am a witness to let everyone know that God is close to the broken hearted. He can and will heal the wounds.

Healing takes time. Wholeness is an act of faith. His word stated that every tear we cry is precious to Him, and they are bottled up, especially out of hurt, pain, abuse, misuse, rejection, and suffering for His sake.

Don't ever give up on God. He knows all, and He sees all. He can take your brokenness and use it for His glory. He can hide every scar, cut, bruise, and past hurts so that they can never haunt you again. He can do the impossible. You must trust Him with your whole heart, love Him with all your heart, mind, body and soul, and believe that He is a Rewarder of those that diligently seek Him.

Enjoy my journey of overcoming the life of depressed, damaged, stained, unclean – from shattered pieces to sacred peace that only God can provide. Even a cracked pot can be used to help other things grow!

Introduction:

When something is broken, we tend to throw it out. Or maybe it is placed in a corner or just simply ignored, despite possibly walking by it every day. There's no use for broken things. They only take up space and cause clutter. Broken things are an eye-sore in the room. When others see broken things in your life they wonder, "Why is she holding on to this old thing? It's useless." "She is a hoarder. Why doesn't she just get rid of it?" Well, it is easy for the person not owning it to decide the destiny of the brokenness. From the outside looking in, no one knows the value of the brokenness. No one knows the memories behind the brokenness. No one understands the pain at stake to get rid of the brokenness. When it is something you can hold or look at, it is easy to decide on what to do with the item.

What about when the broken item is a person? Maybe the person does not look as though there is a problem. By the grace of God, He preserved the outer appearance to keep the wrong people away due to the vulnerability. How can you determine the brokenness within a person? What causes brokenness in a person? What are the characteristics of brokenness? Why is it so hard to release the pain of brokenness? Is there truly hope for someone in shattered pieces? Can God truly restore brokenness, even the years lost?

From my journey, you will see that God's Word is still the same. It has power. I truly believe the Bible. Is there anything too hard for God? Ephesians 3:20 is one of my favorite scriptures: Now unto Him that is able to do exceedingly abundantly above all that I can ask or think, according to the power that works in me (paraphrased with emphasis).

This is not about a crack in the ceiling nor a bad experience from someone stepping on your toes. This is for those who have been broken to a state of beyond repair physically and mentally, yet in the spiritual aspect, the peace that has been found makes everything worth the journey. This is to help others understand that brokenness can result in a powerful destiny that can lead to a fulfilled life.

I have taken the broken pieces of my life and given them to God, as I focused on His Word for healing, repair, restoration and wholeness. I am a product of broken marriages, broken childhood, broken jobs, and a broken spirit, **BUT** God never left my side. There were times that I walked away from Him, or I tried. It was because of His loving kindness that I am still here to tell others of His goodness, grace, and mercy.

When the word of God says there is nothing new under the sun, there isn't. The specific details are not the same, but the overall experience or root of the issues is nothing new to God. I am not the first to experience brokenness, and I am truly not the last. I can be an advocate for those who are broken or those who have overcome brokenness. Revelations says that we overcome by the Blood of the Lamb and the word of our testimony. This book is the praise and testimony of part of my journey with Christ as I walked through brokenness. Truth be told: most of the time, the Holy Spirit carried me through the worst, most difficult, and darkest times.

Join me, as I open the wounds of my brokenness and see the deep scars that God has healed from the inside out. In the physical realm, a wound is completely healed when it heals from the inner surface out. God has taken my brokenness, my shattered pieces and reconstructed my hurts, pains, wounds to develop a sacred peace within Him. I am not ashamed of the Gospel of Christ. I am not ashamed of the life behind me. I am grateful and look forward to the life in front of me, because God is saying, "your latter days shall be greater than your former days." "My grace is sufficient." "I will give your double for your shame." "I come that you may have life and life more abundantly." "I will bless those who bless you and curse those who curse you." "Meditate on My Word day and night, and you will have good success."

There are so many scriptures that I have learn to pray to God. He honors His word. As a nurse, I have learned the science of deep wounds and how they heal. As a child of God, I have felt the results of deep wounds and how He alone can heal.

May this book guide you to the Great Physician that can bind up and heal your wounds. Be blessed and be encouraged to know that your brokenness will be healed.

Damaged Goods...

~1~

Predestined for Greatness

As stated in my first published book, <u>The Woman at the Well: from Guilt to Grace</u>, I was destined for greatness. I was born to praise the Lord. My mom told me the story of my arm coming out first during her labor. As a medical professional, I know that is a critical situation, yet she never mentioned having a C-section. She told of the long hours the doctors spent turning me in utero. As I ponder the scenario, I wonder how and why God saved my life that day. As I reminisce from my obstetrician/labor & delivery rotation in nursing school, how was that medically possible? The water was broken. I was pushed back in the uterus with moments to spare. Surely, there should have been some oxygen deprivation. Yet, to God be the glory, I am still here. I am grateful that God allowed me to live, despite some feelings and failures that I have faced. I must be honest and let you know that there were many times, I wanted to die and even attempted suicide. From those foolish acts, I realize that I am here for a reason, and it is more than what I can ever imagine.

The devil, who roars around like a lion seeking to devour me, has been on his job for a long time. He has tried to take me out as a baby, as a young child, as a teenager, and as an adult. I was told that if the devil is not bothering you, you must be on his team. I thank God that even though satan takes time to try to take me off course, so that with the grace of God and the work of the Holy Spirit, he sees that he has a fight on his hands. I am a fighter, and I am a lover. I fight differently now. I fight in the Spirit. The weapons of my warfare are not carnal. They are not of this world, but of the Word. The kingdom suffers violence and the violent takes by force. I have been violated. I'm ready to fight and take back everything the devil stole from me. He is bold enough to come into my life, sit at my table, sleep in my bed, attend service with me, interrupt my job, wreak havoc in my family, and try to slander my name. I am bold enough to go to the throne of grace and ask for whatever I need to eliminate him from my future.

According to Jeremiah 1:5, the Prophet Jeremiah wrote, "Before I formed thee in the belly I knew thee; and before thou camest forth out of the womb I sanctified thee, and I ordained thee a prophet unto the nations." This was the message spoken from God to Jeremiah. I feel as though God still speaks to me from His Word. I am not an ordained Prophet, nor have I been called as a Prophet. I have been called to be an Evangelist and Teacher according to the gifts of the Spirit that Jesus provided for us. During my time of brokenness and healing stage, I thank God for mentors and spiritual leaders who have and are still guiding me to the purpose that God has for me. It is too easy for us to look in the past of someone and write them off or discredit their dreams of what God has told them. I knew as I child that I was destined to move around and spread the Word of God and lead others to Christ. There were times in my life that I allowed someone to take me off course. That will come later in the book.

Remember this, if you forget everything else or never move forward in this book, God has a plan for your life. He already has it written out. Your job is to walk through the journey. There will be times when the journey is dark and hard to travel. There will be times when strength is lost and the will to live is small. There will be days when you must walk alone and trust God when you cannot even trace Him. There will be moments when you feel like you will never find your way and your mind tells you to give up. Through all the turbulence, turmoil, and trials, God is still there! Jesus made a way for you to be reconciled to a great relationship with the Father, and He left the Holy Spirit to guide and comfort you through it all. The race is not given to the swift nor the strong, but the one that is willing to endure to the end. So, don't grow weary in well doing, for in due season, you will reap a harvest. In both passages, the key is don't give up!

One thing that I have learned from my years of living is that God chose me first. He already had a plan in mind for me. He mentioned it in Jeremiah 29:11 and I realized His plan when I was in my late 20's. That was a time when I was having trouble in my marriage. It was a trial that momma and daddy could not fix. It was a troubled time that push me into the arms of a loving God when no human arms could love me enough. It was a time when I could not plan from one moment to the next, and the word of God leaped from the page, "For I know the plans I have for you, declares the Lord, plans to prosper you and not to harm you, plans to give you hope and a future." What? You have a plan, even though my plan did not work. I was chosen to be a good wife, to have children, to keep house and work to help have a better life than our parents did. Now that all of that is over, You have a plan for me? I was strong in the Lord then, yet I was wounded. I was so far away from home. I was determined to be strong during this test of my life. This was a time when I had God to lean on. I was determined to hold on to Him for dear life, literally.

What God has for me is for me. I will never give up on His plan. My destiny has not been reached. I have been damaged, broken, beaten, abused, mistreated, manipulated, molested, raped, and left for dead, **BUT** God is not done. Every day that He allows me to wake up with the power to praise and worship Him, as well as the strength to do what needs to be done without fear, I will love unconditionally as He has commanded me to do. That love begins with loving myself, despite the brokenness, wounds, and scars.

~2~

How the damage occurred

There is always a starting point of how something begins to malfunction or how it is broken. With today's technology and advanced research, it is easy to pinpoint the origin of how something shifted or broke to cause damage in a process or life. Some things occur suddenly and at times, the process can take years to manifest. It can be caused by a known agent or issue, as well as unknown factors that are indirectly involved in your life. Sometimes, brokenness is a repeat of shattered dreams, which I thought it could never happen again or never dreamed it would happen to me. Sometimes, we go into situations thinking we are healed, only to have someone open a wound that was believed to be healed, but it was only covered. There are times when people know of your wounds and they come to remove the covering or safety area to cause infection or further shattering of your life. I have been through it all. I have seen it all. I am a living witness that God can and will heal your innermost parts of the brokenness and make you whole, as you trust Him by faith.

In this chapter, I am discussing some of the issues or circumstances in my life that led to brokenness. While having physical therapy treatment for a torn muscle, the first visit the therapist told me, "I am going to hurt you in the beginning, but by the end of the session, you will feel better. And within eight weeks, you will feel new." I promise before this book is complete, you will visualize the peace that I have found in trusting God during my times of brokenness.

Child molestation

I don't dwell on the mishaps of my life. I thank God that through all the brokenness, He has given me the ability to keep moving and enjoy an abundant life.

I remember this dark time in my life so vividly. It only comes to mind when I need to witness or have discussions on how to overcome. At the age of 4 to 5, I was molested by an adult cousin. He was the baby sitter for my brothers and me, when we were visiting during the summer in New Orleans. It continued for a while after returning to my grandma's house. I never knew why it happened and how it was my fault. I just remember sleeping in my parents' bed one morning and awakening to a heaviness on me. I remember the very first time. I remember the pale blue walls in my parents' bedroom. I remember having my dad's t-shirt on. I remember the layout of the house. I remember that he told me never to tell or something bad would happen to me and him. I remember his breath in my ear and the hardness I felt between my legs. I remember the pain that left me speechless, without a sound. I remember. I cry as I write this, but they are tears of joy to know that I'm still here to tell my story and help others.

I was always small in stature. I took after my grandmothers on both sides. I loved wearing my dad's shirts because it was like a long dress. I would put on my mom's shoes and pretend to model, not even knowing what I was doing. Yet there was a part of me that wanted to follow my brothers and mimic them. I was what some called a tom-boy. There is a difference compared to a lesbian. I never had feelings for females or desiring to have relations with one. I have been asked, but as I told people in college, "I am strictly dickly, no woman can satisfy me sexually." Some desired to challenge me, but I never allowed the enemy to take me there.

My parents were good to us. I don't remember suffering for anything, but now that I am older, I realize that we were considered poor. But my parents and grandparents always made us think we were rich. We still carry those attributes today. We believe in working for what we want, because God promised to supply our needs.

Back to the molestation, I believed the trauma of the act did two things in my life:

1. My innocence was taken, and it is something that I can never get back.

2. It taught me resilience in the face of adversity and to trust God for strength during the worst of times.

No child should have to deal with this type of trauma, trial, or trouble. Could this have led to the numerous divorces in my life? Could it have pushed me into an underlying depression that prevents me from lasting, loving relationships? Why did God allow such a terrible act to happen at that age? How could my parents trust him to care for me? Why didn't I tell someone? No one else had ever treated me this way. What did I do wrong to deserve such a cruel act as a child?

I remember singing my first song in church, at the age of three. I felt like Jesus was right there. I remember crying after the song was over. I sang "Yes, Jesus Loves Me." My grandmother taught it to me. I remember having on a little white dress. And people said how little I was. I stood by my brother and sang. But when it was over, I just cried. I think it was my experience of the Holy Spirit in me, but I did not know anything about the Holy Spirit, at that time.

I do remember learning about Jesus in Sunday School, before the molestation. After the molestation, I looked for Him more. I felt safe in church. Strange! I never saw my cousin in church. But at home, I was quiet. I was obedient. I was scared to get in trouble. I did not want anyone to get in trouble. But over time, it happened again, and again. I had no concept of time. But I had a concept of pain, physically and emotionally. I started to talk to myself and have imaginary friends. Friends that would never hurt me. This was the beginning of my brokenness.

Bullying

As time passed, not knowing one day from the next nor having any concept of time, I remember summer from winter and time for school to start. I was terrified. I did not want to leave grandma. I was not really safe at home, but I was safe with her, when she was home. The molestation led to shyness and timidity – both ungodly attributes of brokenness. Some people think shy people are cute. To be honest, shyness is a form of nervousness, reserve, timid, withdrawn, repressed type of way for someone to say that I am not confident in myself; I have something to hide. To the person viewing the shy one, it is their way to show dominance and/or find ways to take advantage of the vulnerability.

As time progressed, I had to attend school. I remember having a tutor at the age of three. My grandmother was an English major, but she had a friend who would visit a bring lessons over to teach me to read and write. I loved playing school. I remember hearing my grandmother and her friend speaking good things over me. They would always encourage me to do great things in life. Even when I was in high school and college, it was the elderly women that encouraged me to do well and showed me how a lady is supposed to act.

As I went to school, people use to call me names and say I was stuck up or I thought I was better than everyone else. I was a slow developer. I was always teased by boys and girls, mostly blacks. I was shy or quiet from head-start up until high school. I wasn't one to fight nor cause trouble. I just wanted to do what was expected and get home.

There was always some that wanted to challenge me. I thank God that I never bowed to the pressure. I had a couple of mishaps in school, but I was never one to get caught up in mess nor starting trouble for anyone. I was talked about and pushed to the limits many times, but I never put myself in harm's way. People called me scared. I was dared at times to fight. But something in me would not allow me to stoop to the level of their attempts. I focused on school and having good grades.

Please do not think that I did not have friends. I had my neighborhood friends. We would hang out at school at times, but mostly, we saw each other as we walked the roads in Mt. Pleasant or at church. As we reminisce, we all have some shortcomings growing up in our little community, but we still have fun and think of the good times we all had growing up. Yet, many were not aware of my secret. I was never good enough for everyone. My brokenness continued through school.

I grew up in a home where my grandfather was harsh, strict. He was so tall. I always thought his head touched the ceiling. As I got older, I realized that he was more than 6 feet tall. He had a deep voice that would shake the entire house, when he was mad. I never heard him yell at my grandma, but he could scare the hell out of all of us if we made her upset. He would threaten us with a gun or a whip or whatever was nearby. I watched him abuse my youngest brother, as he kicked him around the house. He shot in my brothers' bedroom one Sunday morning because they were not ready for church when my grandmother told us all to be ready. He came out and asked if anyone was in there. When we called one brother's name, he stated, "well, he's dead." I was scared that day, but I never remember crying.

It was nothing for us not to show emotion. We did not go around saying "I love you." We always heard how ugly we were or how we looked like monkeys. It became a joke. But he would always call me his "lil yellow gal." My brothers said he was not trying to hurt me, but when bullets would fly, I did not see any name on one of them. I ran with the pack. I thank God that none of the stray bullets ever hit any of us.

My grandmother was quiet, mild, meek, not even five feet. But she would control him, not in the physical way. She would pray, and he would cower down. She always taught me to fight in prayer. I never understood it. I watch my granddad, momma, and daddy beat folks and curse them out to scare the mess out of them. I wanted to be like that. But I did not receive those traits. I did endure some negative things that hurt me emotionally. Some words spoken that I was mature enough to know that God would take care of the problem. I remember praying about everything. Grandma said, "no matter what it is, God sees it all and He hears it all. Just pray and allow Him to take care of people."

I never understood how the one's you loved were the ones that would speak such horrible things to you and about you. But through it all, God kept me and strengthened me through the brokenness. One thing I know, you cannot control how people treat you.

Lack of control

In the previous book, I discussed how gambling was an issue in my family. I remember playing cards and shooting dice, at an early age. When I say early, I mean as early as three years of age. My grandmother did not believe in gambling. She would always talk to us about going against God. We, as children did not gamble in public, just mostly in the house when our parents were present, or our grandfather had us play. My grandmother would fuss, but she never harped on it. I remember when I played, I would give her all my winnings to pay a bill. I don't know what I knew about bills, but my family laughs today about me giving grandma the money when I won.

This addiction led to me losing control as an adult with gambling at the casinos. I was so caught up one time, I lost more than $1000 in a few hours. I was hooked on poker and blackjack. I was delivered for more than seven years, until my last marriage. The stress of another broken marriage led me to lean on gambling again. I am not blaming him, nor his shortcomings for my sin. I just know I reverted to familiar spirits that were not godly, but at the time, it felt good! It was my escape. I regret it many times and I repented. I must say, now, once again, I am delivered. I used to bargain with God and say, "well, at least I am not cheating." My husband thought I was sleeping with people on the job. But the Holy Spirit revealed that gambling was still sin! We try to justify our sin with rationalizing. The word says that if you know to do right and you don't, it's sin. (paraphrased).

I never stopped tithing. I never missed paying bills. But the money I used for "entertainment" (as I put it), could have been used for Kingdom building. I can be transparent and thank God for protecting me in my mess. I used it as my escape to hide from accusations. I lost control of who I was and Who I represent. I made excuses. I sinned against God. I am reaping the consequences.

Self-control is a fruit of the Spirit. When one segment lacks, they all are tarnished. We cannot pick and choose what part of the fruit to represent. It all works together for the good. We are accountable for our actions. My lack of self-control led to brokenness. This is a part of my life that I caused. I shattered the dreams and delayed the outcomes that God had for me, BUT I praise Him that He has not given up on me. I repented; and I am forgiven.

Too trusting of people

I have always had the personality of trusting people first, until they hurt me. Then I will never trust them again. The word of God says to "trust no man." It also says, "Trust in the Lord with all of your heart..." But I always go forward head first without really counting the cost. I lead by emotions. I so want to be loved by everyone. I don't like to hurt people. There were plenty of times that I would rather hurt, or I would cover up or run away from a situation to protect someone else. I just thought that I would eventually heal or get over it, because of Who God is to me. Not realizing that the enemy would many times place people in my life to take advantage of the opportunity. I have gotten to a point now that I cannot, nor will I take responsibility for someone else's actions. I am not Jesus. I am an ambassador for Him. I did not hang on the cross and die for anyone. I have no power to save anyone, I just have the ability to tell others of His goodness.

I have allowed others to take advantage of my kindness and gentleness. This had happened for years, by many in different positions and economical status, from all backgrounds and nationalities, religious and nonreligious. I must say, the ones that hurt me more were church members. Notice, I did not say Christians, but church members. Christians do not hurt each other. I had to back away from some people because they took my size and kindness for granted. Lost some friendships because they challenged my faith. Lost some marriages because they said, "the Bible said a woman is supposed to submit to her husband." And 'likewise' was always left out! But trusting others instead of trusting God led to my brokenness.

Evil motives of others

I am just an old-fashioned, yet well-educated country girl. I have traveled many places within the United States and visited three other continents. I never have and never will try to trick people nor manipulate others. I was taught to work hard for what I wanted and to keep God first in everything I do. I was taught that what you do to others will come back on you. I was terrified to misuse people.

It wasn't until later in life that I truly experienced the evilness, I mean the spiritual attack of the enemy through someone else. In the last two marriages, the physical and spiritual abuse that has increased is a revelation of the word that talks about the demon leaving and the house being sweep and returning to find the house clean, then going out to return with seven demons stronger. (paraphrased from Matthew 12:43-45). I allowed the enemy in because I did not take counsel, nor did I obey God's word. I was looking for and expecting someone to love me for me and accept my past. I wasn't hiding anything, anymore. But some people enjoy the vulnerability of others. They use it as a weakness to manipulate and abuse you as they try to get ahead and take all you have. They pretend to love God and quote scriptures and the next thing, you're sucked into their web of deceit and trying to ruin your reputation and character.

How could someone you live with, put your trust in, share most intimate time with be the enemy that you never expected? Why was I put in this situation? What did I do to deserve this? I thought a man was supposed to protect his wife, his queen, his home. You knew your motives when you sought me out. You played games and tried to keep me from knowing true love. But what you did not know: I knew God before I knew you. I know what true love is. I know God to be love. It would be different if I did not know God. But bless the Lord, it backfired!!! You will reap what you sow. I was shattered, but you never broke me with this tactic. I am back on the Potter's wheel!

Jealousy

Now this is one that is difficult to get rid of and it comes with so many schemes, tactics, manipulation and maybe even death. I am not talking about women being jealous of how your look, your size, your job, or the way your carry yourself. I am specifically talking about in your marriage. This can be in your relationship and you are not even aware until years have passed, especially when your spouse is in the church and in ministry. We look good out in public, or we did. There was always competition. If I pray, he had to pray louder and longer with bigger words. If I sing, he had to sing louder and tell me where I messed up or sometimes, belittle me when others compliment me. If I join a ministry, he had to join and try to take charge. If I volunteer in the community, he tried to outshine me. Even to the point of doing what I love, nursing, he tried to tell me how to do my job, something that I have been doing for almost 30 years.

When we were in public, he seems to praise my actions unless it was too good. But in private, he would tell me how God would not answer my prayers, or how I made a mess of things in service, or how I was inappropriately dressed. Things to make me second guess my relationship with God. He would tell me how I would praise too loud or I should keep quiet on certain issues, especially if I asked a question in Bible Study. He stated that I should come home and get answers from my husband. He would tell me how I believed the pastor over my husband and God wasn't pleased. Yet every time I looked, he was in the pastor's face. I was supposed to be seen and not heard. He would tell men about me, discuss intimate things in Sunday School or class and then accuse me of flaunting in front of men in the church. Then he would talk about how they looked at me. He would respond with "God is a jealous God and I have a right to be jealous of my wife. I will hurt someone over you." That is an evil type of jealousy. God has a right to be jealous over what He made. This man did not make me, nor did he provide, protect or take care of me.

He admitted that he was jealous a couple of times:

1. Because of my career and my success (I had been doing my career for almost 25 years when we met) I believed in Matthew 6:33
2. The relationship I had with my family, especially my son (he felt that I should not help my child to succeed, at 18 they should be on their own)

My question: how has things worked for you? Because you chose not to take advantage of opportunities offered, I was supposed to give up everything? Because you chose to not sacrifice for your children, I was supposed to just turn my back and tell my son, have at it, when he was still attending school and working? I never asked him to sacrifice anything for me. But he saw fit to let me know when I was not sacrificing, or he did not feel I was sacrificing for him.

The result:

- try to ruin my reputation
- tell lies to anyone who listens
- tell secrets that I confided with him
- show disloyalty

- have affairs and compare me to others
- leave when things didn't go his way
- physical and spiritual abuse
- using social media to compete
- flirt in my presence to try to make me jealous, gets angry when I am not
- accuses me of affairs
- inconsistence in word and deed
- does not keep promises
- would not help with bills

This became my worse part of brokenness. It was hard to pin-point and more difficult to separate and heal. The devil thought he had me, but I got away, thanks to the help of the Holy Spirit that covers me.

Rape

As stated in the first book, I have been raped twice. I was asked for forgiveness 10 years after the first happened. The second one, when I was leaving work late one night. The hardest part was the police telling me that they had the guy and they did not believe me. They released him, even though he gave me a false name and identity. But God is dealing with everyone involved. I have forgiven him as well. But the brokenness I endured could never be repaired. I felt like the little girl again.

I never thought it was possible to be raped by your husband. It wasn't that I did not love my husband, but the way he used scripture (perverted) to justify certain things that I was to do as a wife. His two favorite:

1. Hebrews 13:4 "Marriage is honourable in all, and the bed undefiled: but whoremongers and adulterers God will judge."
2. 1 Corinthians 7:5 "Defraud ye not one the other, except it be with consent for a time, that ye may give yourselves to fasting and prayer; and come together again, that satan tempt you not for your incontinency."

I love the Word. It is a lamp unto my feet and light unto my path. So, I guess you are thinking that he was correct in these scriptures. Yes, but what was the motive? When we had been separated for months or even a year, he expected me to just allow him to come in and have sex without knowing who he had been with. I know one thing about him, he is a sex addict. He has made it known. He has stated that others have approached him. And with all the accusing, I know he has obliged, especially if a woman challenged him. I know my husband. So, going for months at a time without it, then bragging about the opportunities, why would I keep opening myself for potential diseases? He would preach this to me so much, I would just give in. Sometimes, I would cry. I would do what God said, "Don't deprive him."

Then, the Hebrews one. Lord, I prayed so much. He would say that everything was honorable in the bedroom, whether I liked it or not; whether it hurt or not. I would go along to keep peace. Sometimes, my health was jeopardized and when I mentioned it, he would say that my prayers would not be heard because I was not honoring God's word. I was confused. I did so much when he wanted, sometimes, how he wanted, but it was never enough. Then when I tried new things, like taking him to an adult store to try new things, not porn, but just toys, he accused me of using them on others. I could not win for losing. The worst thing he did, other than physically hurt me, was to compare me to other women he had. Lord, why? In the heat of passion, I did not want to hear what he had done with others. What would he say if I compared him with another man? I asked God to give me amnesia on my past, but he seemed to think I needed a mental picture of his escapades. I was broken and had to endure more cracks every time I connected with him. Then to have to converse about other events by asking questions… "is this the best you've had?" What? All I cared about was what I had right now. I could care less about what I had before. It was irrelevant. What pain to endure. Should I have broken him and answered inappropriately? I would never do that. I truly love him. Even with all my brokenness, I prayed. I fasted. I was patient for years, even through all the revolving in-and-out tactics.

Lord, if this is what your word means, help me to overcome the enemy's tactics. How can I overcome this pain, emotionally, mentally, physically, and spiritually?

Is our marriage really honoring you? Am I being disobedient? Are You truly ignoring my prayers, especially when they are for the good of our marriage and family? Help me understand. Help my unbelief. Increase my faith.

Abuse

Abuse comes in many forms. I have experienced it all in some form or another, by different people, within and outside of the family. It hurts worse when it comes from those you love. As revealed in the first book, <u>The Woman at the Well: From Guilt to Grace</u>, one of my worse experiences of physical abuse lasted for four hours during one episode. I am so grateful that God has protected me from residual and effects of the things I endured. My most surprising episode was while my mom was visiting. Still until this day, he brings up how I abused him. He has acknowledged that he hit me because I hit him. I did not hit him that day. He said he only slapped me. This is another event that I wish to forget. But every now and again, he brings it up and elaborates, but he seems to have amnesia. His account of the event is far off from the event where I was the starring cast member. I still remember the pictures the police took to show the bruises in my face, behind my ear, on my arms, to the back, and no one thought to feel my head – most of the swelling was hidden by my hair. I had hematomas and a concussion. I remember going to the Emergency Room, and the guy cried with me as I explained what happened. This is another event in my life that hurts to write. But the tears are cleansing. The five minutes I suffered from fist blows and attempts to guard my head, felt like hours. I thought I would die, but I could not allow my mom to deal with my drama. Having her present was the worst feeling of my life.

Physical abuse is the quickest way to break a person's heart, dreams, goals, and spirit. As we attempted to reconcile, I kept believing that God would bless the relationship. I gave up friends. I cut off communication with some family. I stopped doing ministry of visiting the elderly. I cut back on going to church. I changed jobs and decreased traveling. I even had him ride along with me. At times, I would drive 10 hours a day to prevent from staying overnight (and my job called for extensive traveling). I did not want anything to give him ideas that I was cheating. I never put myself in a position to cheat, but he felt that I did, and he accused me frequently, especially if I was too tired for intimacy. Many times, I would come home late only to be interrogated and still had to cook because he was home all day and waited for me to come in to cook.

The abuse was no longer physical. According to him, he was laying hands on me to pray for me, as he choked or forced me in certain positions that led to restraint. Then it turned into emotional and mental abuse, where he was telling things about me to people in the community and the church. Eventually, financial abuse began. He refused to help with bills. He stated that he would not take care of me so that I "can take care of a grown man" (referring to my son). I was speechless. I told him to leave because he was not willing to help me pay bills and take care of his child. He asked for two weeks. I granted it. I thought that was the worse that I could endure, until the enemy gave me even more. We went on a cruise. He promised to pay half since we were separated. He never reimbursed me but went on the cruise and made my last four days a living hell! He told me that I haven't done anything for him and I meant nothing to him. When it was time to get off, he owed the ship money for charging on his card. He did not even have the money to pay it. My flesh wanted to walk away and leave him standing there, since I did not do anything for him. But I paid the balance. Once again, when we were in the car, I was talked about, scolded for not being a wife and a good mother. At this point, he wasn't abusing me, I was abusing myself. Nowhere in the Bible does it say that I am supposed to endure such evil treatment.

Ok, God! I get it. He doesn't love me. But I kept going back when he was at his lowest. When our daughter was ill, (well his daughter, because he reminds me that she is 'his child') he told me not to come the hospital because I was the enemy. Because I notified her family of her illness. All of this was a week before the cruise. That was my time from God to cut him from the trip, but stupid me, a glutton for punishment. I allowed him to go on the trip. He left his child a week after getting out of the hospital. But I realize, I wasn't the only one being abused. I could not protect her like I should have. I finally released myself from the agony of imprisonment.

Well, with physical and financial abuse comes emotional and mental abuse. The degrading started. The comparisons of other women asking to sleep with him. The boasting of having many to choose from. Telling me what women tell him. The reports of information, wrong information, going through the church. All I could say was pray and watch the fruit. He was charming, handsome and has a gift of gab. I wasn't competing with my husband. Just when I thought the enemy had nothing else to throw at me, the curve ball from hell came - talk of a pregnancy in the church. I asked him because legally we were married. Months later, I was in the middle of a mess that caught me off guard and it revolved around something that he said. I don't talk about anybody but my own mess. If I don't have proof, I do not discuss. If I need to know something, I go to the source. But when you cannot confide in your spouse, why have a union? There is nothing within it that leads to unity. What have I sown to reap this mess? What sin am I in or committing to cause this much drama in my life? I have repented for things I did not do and asked for unknown sin to be revealed. Lord, disloyalty was the worst thing to cause brokenness and then to lie further to church people. WOW!!! I was ready to give it all up. I was defeated. Lord, you even revealed truth to me. I did not take heed. I kept wanting a relationship from a man who really did not want me.

The shocking part, believe it or not, church folk took his side. They soothed his wounds, stroked his ego and I was left to fin for myself. For months, I watched as so-called church folk changed their attitude towards me. I felt like an outsider. I heard of some things that were said. I confided in two people to pray for me for strength and endurance. The others, I was just cordial and loving. I stayed committed to ministry and to God's plan. I knew my season was over. I was damaged in every way to include spiritually.

He told me, "God is going to take everything you have." My question to him was, "why would God do that?" But I started to believe it. I was grateful that God took him first so that he could not see all the broken pieces that resulted from his abuse, his manipulation, his lies, his jealousy, his games, his spiritual conduct, but most of all my condoning it.

See in a later chapter how sometimes, we must give it all up to get it all back, and then some!

~3~

Shattered pieces lead to lack of fulfillment

As a child of God, we should never feel inadequate by anyone's standards. The Bible is the <u>b</u>asic <u>i</u>nstructions <u>b</u>efore <u>l</u>eaving <u>e</u>arth. If it is not in God's word, then it is not relevant to living. We do not have to keep getting along to get along! If it is not love, you can tell. When it causes you to stop loving yourself or your family, or it leads to shame, it is not a relationship for you.

Feeling of inadequate or not good enough

I have had moments that I never feel adequate or good enough, because of my own choice or from what someone said. The adage that "sticks and stones may break my bones, but words will never hurt me" is a lie. Words hurt, and the wounds are not seen. At least with physical abuse, the visible wounds will heal, on the surface. No one takes time to look beyond the surface. It is so important for Christians to be careful in their attitude and how they treat newcomer's or visitors at the church. Sometimes, they judge what they look like on the outside. We never know what a person is going through at that moment or during their season of life. Everyone is different, and everyone deserves to be loved.

I realized that the reasons for my brokenness came from people and situations that were broken. Some people prefer to hurt others rather than seek help or reveal their flaws and start the healing process. Each shattered piece of my life has pushed or pulled me to Christ. I wish I could have done some things differently or made better choices, but I was given this life to live and I did what I thought was best so many times.

Now I stated pushed or pulled because, there were times when I was catapulted into the plan God had for me or redirected by a dragging-type feeling. Whatever worked to get me back on the right course, I appreciate. I realized that if things had not happened the way they did, I would still be in the situation taking the same abuse. Like the Israelites, going in circles, allowing a 30-minute journey to take years to overcome.

I spent months in my townhouse confused and believing that God was punishing me for something I did not do. I believed the lie that satan told me. I was trusting in a relationship with a man and gave up on the best relationship I had ever known, all my life. I fasted for days, waiting to hear from God. I prayed, but I did not hear from Him. Then my job started to suffer. My boss told me to pray, yet he was also telling me to get over it. Basically, he stated to get myself together or there would be consequences. What was I to do? I was allowing a revolving door to be attached to my heart. The ultimate betrayal, but he would come back when he desired sex from me and then leave within an hour or sometimes spend a night, only to leave early morning. Or he would stay long enough to bring up issues that I thought we had dealt with, just to cause chaos. Or would tell me about women that were fighting over him or him "fighting sharks everyday to get to work." I was confused. Lord, why? What am I doing wrong?

I started to lose my passion to sing, to praise, to worship. I stopped praying. I was holding on by attending Bible study. But I was drained. I had an inward battle that only the pastor and my professor were aware of. I asked for prayers of deliverance. But all I got was, "I'm praying for you, just hold on." Hold on to what? A curse spoken over me by someone I trusted, loved, gave my all for? I could not find God's hand. Where was He during my time of darkness? How was I to bounce back from this? Then I realized that God was never the blame. He was faithful, and I thank Him for His mercy.

Always take the blame to keep the peace

With every encounter, I allowed him to visit when he desired. I answered his calls. I kept listening to the negative comments, the lies of my being the worst mom and wife. I had forgotten about the God of my salvation. I was listening to a man that I wanted to be a god for me. He turned things around to make me look like the villain and he was the victim.

I was always apologizing for doing any and everything wrong, even when I did nothing wrong. I was apologizing for my past when I did not even know him. I was apologizing for an affair that I did not have, one that he conjured up in his mind and believed. And I apologized to keep the peace. But there was no peace, just pieces of my dream shattered and no way possible to put it back together. The more I tried to make it right, the more I was treated like I was just a woman in the night. It was basically driven by sex.

Then I started to have symptoms of my worse fear – sexually transmitted disease. Thank God it was just a basic yeast infection. But I realized the danger I was putting myself in. In these days, just a kiss can lead to oral cancer because someone chooses to have oral sex with someone else. He started to ask why I did not kiss him like I use to. I was scared. I did not want the effects of someone else introduced in my life. He did not trust me and that was probably because he was doing so much himself.

I talked about competing on social media earlier. I was monitoring his page and I realized he had two Facebook accounts. I had access to one and was restricted to certain things and could not view anything from the other. I was always mentioning how things were not appropriate for a minister and how he commented on certain posts. I discussed about etiquette and bombarding other's posts and making it his, with his pictures and graphics, that always included or turn someone's else post into his. To him, he was winning souls. But I was getting messages and private calls from taunting to complaints. I had to block some people. Sometimes, when I would confront him, it was a reason for him to change a privacy setting or to block me. As usual, I apologized to keep the peace. I stopped looking for his page, but then I realized he was going through mine, which was public. I hid nothing. I can't hide from God, I had no reason to hide from him. I was accused of having an affair so many times. But I did not block him, until he decided to block me. Well, I got off social media for a while. When he blocked me, he was too proud to ask for a friend request, again. But I was blocked from every access. It was ok. I did it before, so tit-for-tat was the game he would play. It wasn't that serious to me. The less I knew the better things would be. I never tried to control him, and I was not about to start now. Social media can lead to brokenness. Be prepared!

Inability to love self

It is hard to love yourself when you are shattered. A crack in the surface leads to seepage or loss of contents. I had lost my passion to dance, sing, praise and even worship. I was in a sad state. I was distant from God. During my dark times, I preferred a marriage filled with lies, disloyalty, betrayal, and misery to serve a God that had all I need to make a life. I made a choice to put a wrecked marriage before God. I did not have a covering.

I had to move. I had lost my ability to love me, because I lost me. I did not know who I was or what my purpose was. I was caught up in giving myself completely to someone who had no intention of giving me anything in return.

It wasn't until I was preparing to leave and return to the home that I left - A home of peace, love, joy, patience, faithfulness, gentleness, goodness, meekness, and temperance – a home that I opened the door to allow the enemy to invade my life, my space, my entire being. I started to regain strength when I volunteered, well, involuntarily assigned to teach a discipleship class on "What on Earth Am I Here For?" I was faithful to do what I was assigned to do. I would drive from one state to another to complete my assignment. I would attend church early on Sunday and attend three services, even if I did not sing or serve. No one knew I was traveling five hours to make it on time for 0730 every Sunday for 3 months. I was just that committed, but God was just that faithful. It was during my drive times that I reconnected with God. I came to know my purpose again. I found me, because God was never lost. I was lost. I was saved and knew God at an early age. I allowed someone with no power to consume my life, my dreams, my destiny and did not contribute to enhancing my life but was determined to destroy my life any way possible.

Jesus said to love your neighbor as you love yourself (paraphrased – Matthew 22:39). When you cannot love yourself, the love Jesus commanded is warped. It is like the passage of "husbands love your wives as Christ loved the church...so ought men to love their wives as their own bodies. He that loveth his wife loveth himself. For no man ever yet hated his own flesh; but nourisheth and cherisheth it, even as the Lord the church" – Ephesians 5:25,28-29. Where is the love? Maybe I did not deserve it. Maybe my shattered pieces were too much to bare. Maybe I was destined for what I received. Maybe it was never meant for me to have a husband. It is not because I do not know how to be a wife. It is because I open my heart to the wrong people who see me as an object and not a representation of God. It is because I settled for someone below the standards of God hoping that he would live the life he talked about.

Low self-esteem because of shame

I was being facetious in the last few sentences above. I learned many years ago that God had plans for me. His word says there is no good thing that He would withhold from me. He also said that it is not good for man to be alone. But He never told me to hook up with some of the filth that I got involved in. I realize that I had a low self-esteem about myself, because of the things spoken to me. I suppressed the negative feelings and allowed them to overshadow my potentials, my dreams, my plans, my walk with God. I allowed sin into my life; and I lost trust in God and shifted to a human that did not care about himself nor me. I allowed the breaking to occur. I knew the Word. I knew what a real man was supposed to do in a marriage, in a family. I knew the order God placed in the family. I knew the vision He had for me. I knew my gifts. I understood my purpose. But like Eve, I was approached subtly, numerous of times. I trusted in the wrong thing with all I had. I lost focus of my Savior and gave the reigns to someone who pushed me to sink; who dragged me into darkness where he was comfortable. When I lost focus, I was filled with shame. Want to quickly be put to shame? Go to Facebook. Look at Snapchat. Read all the hurtful comments and craziness on Twitter. Check out the selfishness on Instagram. Social media, if not used properly, can cause destruction and chaos.

Shame has caused me to isolate myself and play into the enemy's trap! Thank God for prayer warriors that don't just pray, they act! I AM not my many marriages or divorces. I AM not the molestation from my childhood. I AM not the rape victim from the past. I AM not the disappointments or lack of achievements that society has placed on me! I AM not my doubts and fears! I AM not a religion, color, size, or shape! I AM naked, but not ashamed! I have taken off the old clothes and put on the new! I have been filled with good fruit, Godly fruit that will live throughout eternity! I AM REDEEMED! I AM a Godly woman filled with the Holy Spirit that causes me to love, live, and encourage!!! I AM the product of a risen Savior that gave His life so that I may live, not just to get by, but live abundantly. I AM a believer destined for heaven. I WILL glorify my Father in all I do, because it is through His grace that my broken, beat-up body is strong enough to continue this journey!

Fear of loving or being loved

I still have some healing to endure. I want to get to wholeness. I want to be in a loving relationship with a man that will have no fear of my past. Yet he will love me as Christ loves me. Because that is how I will choose to love whomever God allows to find me. I will never give up on a loving relationship. I have too much compassion to give up.

At one time, I felt inadequate. I felt incompetent. I felt less than a woman. I was afraid of loving again, or really being loved. My first husband told me I would never be happy. My last husband told me that God was going to take everything. In either situation, I prayed that neither would see me at my worst. God has always brought me before great people and provided success. It takes prayer and fasting to overcome such harsh comments from people you love. But I am here to tell you that God can heal brokenness. The Potter wants to put you back together again. Keep seeking Him. Draw close to Him. When you are weak, He is strong. His strength is perfect. His ways are not for me to understand, but to obey. I have learned how to lean and depend on Jesus.

~4~

Along the journey

The journey was never promised to be easy. There are so many choices in life, so many trials we must endure, so many distractions and decisions to help determine our fate in life. Maybe you never questioned your decisions. There have been many of times I wondered "what if?" after making specific decisions. I had some good days. I had some hills to climb. I had some weary days and some restless nights. But as I look around, and I think things over. All my good days outweigh my bad days, I won't complain. I am sure many of you have heard the verse to the song, "I Won't Complain." I have learned to be content in whatever state I am in. This song ministered to me in the time when my dad passed. I sang it at his funeral, because that was the last thing he spoke to me on the phone – "I won't complain."

Walking away too soon

There have been times in my life when I felt as though I gave up too soon. But not this time. I felt I held on to the wrong thing at the wrong time, which almost cost me everything I work so hard for. I am not talking about the material things in life, I mean the prayers prayed to keep me sane and strong in the Lord. Prayers that were requested to have a closer walk with God. If anything, I walked away from God too soon. Believing that I could trust in human efforts because of some quoted scriptures. I forgot the devil knows scripture. The key is the fruit that is produced. I should have been focusing on the visual of what was produced instead of what was being said. Sweet nothings are just what it is – NOTHING!

There is one relationship I regret walking away from too soon. Only God and I will ever know the true value of what I lost. I am a true believer that all things work together for the good. This is not a relationship that was built on lust, but at my young age, I did not know nor understand how precious true love was. It was the love of knowing a real Savior. A relationship based on unconditional love. One that if I had stayed the course, I would not have endured the pain and suffering that I have gone through. I would have made better choices in life. I would have saved myself some unnecessary heartache.

I made a huge mistake to put any man before God. I know the order that God ordained. The word, "submit" has never been terrifying to me, even though, I have been accused of not knowing how to submit. According to Webster's definition, submit means to accept or yield to a superior force or to the authority or will of another person. God's order, as we have been taught many times is God, Christ, man, woman, children. As stated in Ephesians 5:22, "wives, submit yourselves unto your own husbands, as unto the Lord." "As unto" is an adverb and preposition, which states to the same degree or extent and in relation to. So, when God is first, I will obey His command to submit, because when I see my husband, I should see Jesus or God in Him. It's difficult to submit to inconsistency, non-Christ-like characteristics, but sometimes, you go against the grain and do what is necessary for peace and not personal gain. First Corinthians 7:3 says, "Let the husband render unto the wife due benevolence: and likewise, also the wife unto the husband. "Likewise" is a term that means in the same way; in like manner; to reciprocate. It starts with the man, the husband, and likewise also the wife. It's hard to reciprocate something that has not been done. But I had to sometime look past the man and focus on God.

My question to myself: Did I give up on God too soon? Could He still work a miracle? Will He still intervene, or will my prayers go unanswered? He knows what's best for me. Although, my weary eyes cannot see. So, I'll just say, "Thank You, Lord!" I won't complain.

Return to the pain

I heard a sermon by a former pastor called "When Enough is Enough." There is nowhere in the Bible that states anyone should remain in an abusive situation. But how do you know when enough is enough? As I listened that day to two sermons and purchased the CD, I realized that I was trying to step into God's position. I kept returning to painful situations when my husband told me that he never believed we would work. He mentioned on many occasions how he kissed me or made love to me and felt nothing. Yet I felt like I had something to prove. I was determined not to have another failed marriage. I was not the one failing. I was forcing something that the head told me would never be. **AND** I ignored the signs. I put myself in a position to be hurt, misused, abused, and manipulated.

When he needed me, I was there. I kept returning to his beckoning call; no matter what it was, or what time he needed me. Until one day, he would deliberately not work, and he lost his car. Twice I helped to pay to catch up and prevent repossession. Day-to-day, I worked and returned home to find him asleep or sitting at the table reading the Bible and complaining. For years, I never said anything. But this was a cycle. He had left me twice before. We agreed that the past was behind us. We were starting over in a new city, well, I was already here for a year and he was coming back, after living here for about three months. When I knew he was returning, I tried to do things that would surprise him. I bought a pillow that had "Hello Handsome" and put it on the bed. When he arrived, the question I received was, "who did you buy this for?" What?! Not, I'm glad to be home or let's do what is needed to make this marriage work. Lord, I need You to shake him up for me. You know I have not done anything.

I spent countless hours, days, nights, weeks, months, and years crying, praying, fasting and clinging to hope that things would turn around. I reached out to any and every one that knew prayer and believed in deliverance from evil spirits and strongholds to pray. One day before our initial separation, he said, "the Holy Spirit told us to fast for 5 days on nothing but water." I admit, I am analytical. I like details. I ask questions for clarification, not for interrogation to make someone feel guilty. Since the Holy Spirit spoke to Him, I asked questions because he stated that I was supposed to fast as well. So, I asked what were we fasting for? For how long during the day? And were we coming together at a certain time? The specific instructions: we started on a Monday, to end Friday from the time we get up until 1800 that evening (that's 6:00p.m. for non-military people). We were to pray at the top of the hour from the time we got up until 1800. At night we were to pray together. Day 1, I called him at around lunch to pray so we would not just sit around thinking about food. When I called, he sounded like he was chewing. I asked, "What are you doing?" He answered, sarcastically, "Eating lunch!" I responded, "but what about the fast? You said the Holy Spirit told you to fast." His response, "I forgot." We hung up. I did not understand it. But I continued with the plan, even though the Spirit had not given me the instructions. That was another cue: If he was not obeying the Holy Spirit, how could he lead me properly?

How could I ever trust a man who doesn't trust God nor believe in Him enough to do what he said he would do.

When I came home daily, I would silence my phone, because I talk to people all day. I did not want to deal with a phone. No one called me except my mom or my son, some friends on occasion, but it was rare. And if they called I would return the call later. I just wanted to focus on him. It was never good enough. He said I was hiding something. The phone was the topic of most of our arguments. I did not cheat even when we were separated. He left me three times, and here I was trying to justify my fidelity. I was subjecting myself to abuse again. If I ignored him, it was an argument. If I tried to defend myself, it was an argument. If I agreed with him, it was an argument. What did I do to deserve this treatment? What seeds did I plant to reap this field of weeds, stickers, thorns? I kept allowing the pain to continue.

Mistrust

I don't believe neither one of us trusted the other. I always told him to trust God, even if he did not trust me. At some point in the relationship, you must trust. But we had none. He did not even trust me with my mom. I started out trusted him, but it was betrayed because of an expectation for him to pay a bill and he chose to misuse funds while I was out of town or away for any length of time.

I did not mean to make this solely about one man, but I never believed he would hurt me worse than any other man had. I confided in him. I confessed all my life issues before we were married. He read diaries that I had from years ago. Things written that I had planned for books and some that I never wanted to revisit ever. He invaded my life and held me hostage to my past. He said he could never forgive me for my past. Well, if God had forgiven me and delivered me, what really could he offer me. He was telling me that he could never love me with all the dirty, stinky, filthy stains that I had, even though I had been washed by the blood of Jesus. He was looking at my past. I was focusing on my future, yet I was allowing him to hold me captive to a time that he was not a part of. His thoughts of me were one of a stranger or criminal that got away with the worst offense ever.

I could never make anyone trust me. I could only live a life that represented the true essence of being trustworthy. Trust does not just happen, it is earned. Even with my child, I have never had to hide money in the house. He has been privileged to large sums of cash for emergency. But never has he just taken any without asking or letting me know he was in need. He earned the right for me to trust him. Even today, he never moves or takes things that do not belong to him. Yes, he is my son, but we have respect for each other's space. Even as husband and wife, should we still have respect for each other's things and space? I was accused of cheating because I use to hand wash my underwear before putting them in the laundry. I was interrogated multiple times for doing that. If I paused while brushing my teeth, I was questioned. If I wore a certain outfit that was too tight, too loose, too colorful, too dark, too light, too secular or too Holy, I was questioned. Even if I was just hanging out at home with shorts and a camisole, I was questioned.

How do you build trust in a relationship? One day at a time. One moment at a time. One event at a time. And sometimes, one thought at a time. It's all about your attitude and how you process things. You must treat others the away you want to be treated.

Buried in your career

Nursing is my career. I truly enjoy what I do to help healing and encouraging people. Nursing is something that I would do for free and have. I love caring for people. I love teaching preventive care. It is a vision that I was given to bring back house calls. I especially want to help educate people with low income, low education, and crisis issues to assist in their care and maintaining their health. I am an advocate, a teacher, a caregiver, an educator, a passionate and patient person for those in their worst of times of illness. I love my role. It reminds me of the slogan for the military: it's more than a job, it's an adventure.

When I started this book, I was in sales. I travelled and did what I loved to do – educating and training physicians, nurses, and lab personnel on use of lab tests and rationale for utilization on a national level. I loved the autonomy of making my own schedule, as long as I was doing the work and having success. The first few years were fabulous. I was single and focusing on success. When I began this last relationship, I had been in sales for over four years and was a nurse for over 20. I enjoyed the travel. There was never a problem until I invited him to a hotel the first year of our marriage. I was conditioned to waking up early in the morning to train before 0630, and I would have training sessions all throughout the day. Usually, I was in an account for one to two weeks at a time all day. I was tired after a long day. I never thought about, nor did I have time to cheat, flirt, or see anyone else. For some strange reason, I was being accused of thoughts he conjured up in his mind. But there was never a problem when I was obtaining trips for President's Club and obtaining lavished gifts. I worked hard so we could play hard. I planned personal trips for us to enjoy abundant life. That never seemed to be good enough. There was always complaining. It was not enough to travel to places he had never been. It became a problem that I was paying for everything. I never complained. I saved so that nothing else would suffer. I planned at the right time and thank God for the President's Club trips to Key Largo, Colorado, Puerto Rico. Because of the hard work as well as the frequent flyer miles and hotel points, in order that we could go to Vegas, Washington DC, Atlanta, Orlando, Honduras, Belize, Cozumel.

But things started to change. He started to become jealous, over sensitive, believing the voices in his ear, instead of the Holy Spirit in his head. He said I cared more about my job than I did him or the family. BULLCRAP!!! I tried to start many businesses with him, so we could work together. I even helped him to start some things he liked. But nothing was ever good enough. He did not want to put forth the effort to be successful. You cannot have a business sleeping in late. You must do things when others are still resting and trying to make something happen. The excuses were wearing thin. I was the only one working. If I stopped, what would happen? I would not be obeying God's will. I applied for local jobs, but nothing ever happened. I felt I was where God wanted me to be.

I was not buried in my career. I was trying to ensure that we never had to live in poverty nor go without. Faith without works is dead. I could not pray for God to bless me financially, while I set at home and just read the word. I had to act on His word and watch it work. If a man doesn't work, he doesn't eat. In my situation, if a woman did not work and cook, she would not eat. BUMMER!! I like to eat. So, I had to do what was needed to bring meat in the house. My job was not my brokenness, but my shattered pieces affected my work setting. The safe-haven that God blessed me to have. I was starting to lose it all. Or that is what the enemy had me thinking.

Lost faith

Maybe you have never experienced a lack of faith. I remember a time in my life when I would never dare challenge my faith in God. Faith of a mustard was all that is required. We are all given a measure of faith. There has come a point in my life when I lost faith. God had not answered my prayers regarding my marriage. He was silent. I could not hear from Him. I know without faith it is impossible to please God. I was so far off course. I wanted something that was not ordained for me. Someone, who could care less about my outcome physically, emotionally, mentally, financially, socially, or spiritually.

I loved him enough to give him his space each time. For the third time, he left. I still had hopes that he would return. And I was willing to accept him in any condition, at any time, despite my emotions. I believed that God could do the impossible. But it wasn't meant to be. Time after time, day after day, I waited, hoping to hear from him. I trusted God to guide me through this. I believed He would bring Him home, but to what? To a place where he was not satisfied. A place where he wanted to make people believe things were good, but in reality, I was never what he desired. I was what he tolerated, until the next one came along. Was that how our relationship came to be? With all that was invested, what did I get in return? I never doubted until I crossed the state line heading back to Texas. He would never visit me unless I would pay for gas or someone else had something else going on in the area. I realized how valuable I was in his life on many occasions, very little.

I finally gave up. I stopped praying. I stopped hoping. I had great memories, but I stopped thinking of good times. I wanted nothing to remind me of him. I started to sell things we had together, which was very little and did not amount to much. I moved things out. I tried to start over, but I became numb. I started to think of all the things I did, all that I gave, all that I endured and suffered. I wanted revenge. I was allowing bitterness to set in. I was losing me. I was replacing God with my agenda and nothing else. What did I have to lose? I was at peace here at home. If I never saw anyone else, I was good. The worse brokenness is when there is no hope. Will I ever have my joy restored? Could I ever have the faith of a mustard seed? I just wanted the pain to go away. A song I loved to hear was "Woman's Work" by Maxwell. It gave me revelation to move on.

Hiding in the church

There were times when I believed the church was the best place to be. And it is. My mom always told me there are two places you should have peace, the church and your home. Well, things are not always the way we want them. But we must understand, the church is like a hospital. So many come in for different reasons. Not everyone has the same issues or symptoms. Some are open to reveal their issues. Others act as though they do not need to be there. Some act as though they have never sinned nor been exposed to sin. Some are in the role of diagnosing your issues and telling you how to live life while their life is in chaos. Some come to get a fix emotionally, like those who seek drugs from the doctor, to give them a high.

My reason was for peace. I found myself in church several days a week. I participated in many ministries and throughout my life, was the leader or chairperson for many. It was my escape. When I wasn't in church, I was at work. And trust me, I was committed. I never allowed church to come before family. I just spent my available time doing something in or with the church. It was what I loved. It was how I was raised. It was a way of life. I found that it was more of a cover-up. It was my alibi of staying out of temptation's way, until temptation hit me in the church.

I thought I was safe. My friends use to tell me that I needed balance in my life. I needed to party and socialize more. I tried it. It wasn't for me. Oh, don't get me wrong, I knew how to party. I could plan a party and people never wanted to go home, but I always felt out of place or guilty, like I was doing something wrong. Somehow, I just did not fit in all the time. I had people in the club telling me that I did not need to be there.

That I was a "good girl" and needed to go home. All this was when I was single.

During my last marriage, we would go out, on occasion. I enjoyed dancing and he enjoyed watching others while we danced. He would tell me who was watching, how they look, and at times what some would say. I started to think that he would set me up to cause confusion when we returned home. He even asked if I was a stripper in my past life. As I shake my head, I could never understand why others saw Jesus in me, but he saw so much bad in me. He called me beautiful yet complained about the way I dressed. I always carried myself in a professional or classy way to represent God and family. I never wanted others to view me in a bad way.

But I thought I was safe in the church. I had to examine myself to truly understand if I was doing God's business or creating busyness? I wasn't a busy-body, I just felt at peace doing whatever I could for the church. I held many positions and serve from local to state levels at different times in my growth. At times, we worked together as a couple. But then, something happened. Either, I was wrong about a scripture or didn't know how to pray right. Or I needed to be taught how to respect my husband in public, according to him.

I was often reminded of the scripture of women being quiet in the church. I discussed that earlier. To him, he stated it was a sign of disrespect for me to try to express my opinion and talk over him. I usually talked when asked a question or when I was teaching. I started to feel like a stranger to God. Why? I don't know, because I knew He was my Friend. He knew me by name. Now, I felt like a stranger. Where did I go wrong? What did I do wrong? Church has become an uptight, ritualistic, place for who competes the best. Compliments led to a competition for us. If I received too many, there was condemnation or consequences. If I hugged a male, I was scolded. If he hugged a female, he was consoling or witnessing. Hmmm. I know God knew the truth. I was accused of having affairs or socializing too long with so many men and a few women in the church. Lord, I could not win at just being a child of the King.

I had to watch how I dressed; how I wore my hair; how I sang; how I taught; how I prayed and why I whispered when I prayed at home. One time, I was told that I needed to pray so he could hear what I was saying to God. Then when I prayed out loud, it wasn't right, and God wasn't hearing my prayers. Lord, I need this brokenness to go away. There is nothing too hard for You, but I was being consumed by a spirit that I did not know.

To leaders in the church: Please, I beg you! PLEASE, know your sheep. Understand their needs. There are signs of abuse. Recognize them. Don't just pass over them because one can speak well, loud, and/or articulate scripture. Look for good fruit being produced. I heard something from my pastor in a workshop: "the emptiest house, speaks the loudest!" Selah!

From Shattered Pieces...

~5~

Your past is not your destiny

Now we are coming to the middle part of the book. Chapter 5. Five is the number of grace. There is hope. God is always standing by. This is where hope starts to kick in. It is time to get out of the pity party and dance like you've never danced before. It's time to get off the bench and actively play the game of life. This is your destiny, and no one can reach it, but you!

His will for me

As stated earlier, Jeremiah 29:11 was the scripture that helped me through my major trial of divorce in my late 20's. Even though it has been almost 30 years since that time, the Word of God is still real, powerful, and alive for me. I visited a church in Jackson, MS, while writing this book, and one thing the Pastor stated, "Know how to use the Word. It's the power of God." (I have heard it so many times in my life).

When the enemy would attack in the past, I use the Word of God. When I would have bad thoughts, I thought on things that were true, holy, noble, righteous, of good rapport, that had virtue. When I felt depressed, I put on praise music. When I felt sick or just could not seem to make it through the day, I worshipped the Lord and prayed all through the day.

But when I married the last time, I was taken off course. I stopped believing in my one and only Savior and trusted my husband to carry me and my family, spiritually, according to the word of God. His memorization and dissecting of the word was so impressive to me, but I never took time to watch the fruit in his life that he produced. He talked a good game. He was the master of the word, yet the result was lack, poverty, complaints, fear, misery, pity, pride.

Yet through it all, God still has a plan for me. He has a future, and it is filled with hope. His will is that I live! His will is that I live abundantly. His will is that I obey His commands and reap the benefits of His promises. There are more promises in the Word of God than anyone could ever provide for me. I lost focus. I was sidetracked by the looks and smooth talking. I did not try the spirit to see if it was of God. Lord, I assisted in the brokenness. I opened the entry for the enemy to sit in my life and play with my future. It was subtle. I had no warning that it was coming. Or did I just overlook the warnings?

I know the purpose God has for my life. My daily task is to keep God first and watch Him add everything else I need. I am to pray and thank Him for all He is, has done, will do and is doing. I am grateful that God has allowed me another chance to reach my destiny that He has set. I am deeper in His word than ever. I am drawing nearer to Him. I am thirsting for His righteousness. I am chasing after Him, while His blessings are chasing me. I am grateful for His will. My day is loaded with benefits. My brokenness is mending. It is restoration time!

Where do I go from here?

I go to the Word of God! When I abide in Him and His word abides in me, I am strong. I can ask anything I want, and He will supply. His word says that He will supply my need according to His riches. And He owns everything. I am assured that God knows the plans He has for me. I can only move higher. It has been a rough road. I have learned to depend on Him in every way for everything. I was asked many times, "do you have to use God for everything?" YES! In all things, I choose to include Him; and I must. When I do not, I slip, slide, and/or fall. I was even told that I was too Holy, too churchy…. what is that? I am not perfect and no where near it. I do know that God's word says to "be ye Holy for I am Holy!" I want to be Holy. Just because I am, doesn't mean that I cannot enjoy life. I am living my best life now. I am enjoying life abundantly. I must remain steadfast, unmovable, always abounding in His work.

I do all I can to keep Him first knowing that He will add everything else that I need. This new path I am walking does not mean that I will not make mistakes or make an incorrect decision. It means that I will trust Him to guide me. I will pray without ceasing. I will worship Him in the beauty of His holiness. I will praise Him continuously.

When mistakes happen, I will run to Him with humility and ask for forgiveness and believe that He is a Rewarder because He gives new mercies every day. I do not take God for granted. I know my Redeemer lives. Because He lives I can face any obstacle placed in my path or He will divert me to the best strategy to overcome. But never again, will I live a life that leads to losing my relationship to Him. Without Him, I am nothing.

Hitting rock bottom

I have hit the bottom. I dare not ask God how low can I go? He may show me. But I never dreamed, nor have I ever been so depressed, oppressed, nor possessed as I have been during this particular season in my life. This is supposed to be the golden years. The time between working hard for a great future and having visions of retirement. But I am fighting demons harder in my 50's than I ever did in my 20's, 30's, or 40's. And I guess the hardest part is believing that a Christian man I trusted would be there for me, chose to walk out, even though, I gave all I had, and he took all he could (and wanted more).

The Holy Spirit showed me in the Word, my error that brought me to this point: Matthew 2:28-30, 43-45 – *"But if I cast out devils by the Spirit of God, then the kingdom of God is come unto you. Or else how can one enter into a strong man's house, and spoil his goods, except he first bind the strong man? And then he will spoil his house. He that is not with me is against me; and he that gathereth not with me scattereth abroad. When the unclean spirit is gone out of a man, he walketh through dry places, seeking rest, and findeth none. Then he saith, I will return into my house from whence I came out; and when he is come, he findeth it empty, swept, and garnished. Then goeth he, and taketh with himself seven other spirits more wicked than himself, and they enter in and dwell there: and the last state of that man is worse than the first. Even so shall it be also unto this wicked generation."*

Part of the commentary for verses 43-45 states, "Be warned that returning to a past bondage from which you were once delivered results in deeper bondage." I am a witness to the result of allowing the enemy to come in and take charge. The enemy is not the person, but the characteristics, personality, attitudes exhibited through the person that goes against the Word of God.

The enemy is so subtle. He knows how to lure his prey off course. One thing I have learned during this season, just stay focused and patient on the Word of God. Eventually, the devil's wiles will be revealed and exposed. He cannot hide for long. He becomes restless and impatient. He starts to accuse you. He becomes angry and allows the anger to hurt and abuse others. I warn anyone, do not play games nor team up with the enemy to participate. His words turn to flattery. He speaks good things from the Word of God, but his actions do not represent Who God is in his/her life, nor does the end-product represent the Fruit of the Spirit.

I remember my first physically abusive relationship. I wanted to die. But for some reason, God left me here. He delivered me. He healed me. He kept me in a place of safety. When I was out of the bondage and started to know more about spiritual strongholds, I understood how the enemy was planning to shut me up or take me out. I attended a worship service in the Houston area during a Metamorphous Conference. Pastor Debra Morton was the guest speaker. Her title that night was "Bounce Back!" I remember her stating that when you hit rock bottom, God has a net there to help you bounce back. What a great analogy for my life. Just when I thought I was hitting rock bottom, the Rock catapulted me beyond where I was and made me better, stronger, wiser.

When I decided to return to my house, I remember feeling so ashamed and feared meeting previous friends and neighbors. I knew they would asked how my husband was or where he was. I did not even return to the church we attended. The pain of realizing that I played with the enemy and allowed him to take me off course made me feel like all the teaching, praying, singing, worshipping and praise dancing was all in vain. The worse feeling was knowing that what I endured was worse this time than what I endured through any failed relationship.

I never stopped attending church. I was led to attend where I knew I could receive proper healing and correction in the Word of God. I am not saying the churches I previously attended would not help me heal. But there was too much of my past and hurt there, and God sent me to a place where I could be protected as I am on the course of wholeness. I am in a congregation of people who teach me nothing but the Word of God. They help me to see my error and pray for me to heal. They chastise me and keep me on track with the Word, through the Word and when I leave, I feel such peace. I don't feel condemned nor ashamed. I leave feeling empowered. I feel connected. They help to ignite a passion for life again. They help to equip me and prepare me for Kingdom living. The older women teach the younger women, even when words fall on deaf ears. They provide unconditional love. They remind you of God's goodness, not your past.

When vision is lost

Have you ever lost your way? Or have you ever used the GPS, and it gave you incorrect directions? It can leave you confused and depressed, especially if you have a specific time to arrive at your destination. It is not different in life issues. When you plan your life and you are on track for success and someone else comes along to discourage you and knock you off track. It can be detrimental to your future.

The Word of God says, "without a vision the people perish." I have always had a goal in mind. My parents taught us to be successful. They taught me to plan ahead and count the cost. The Bible mentions counting the cost as well. It is embarrassing to start a project or try to take on a task and not have the ability or the fortitude to finish it. I was never a quitter. Even with other failed relationships, I was determined to do better and not allow a bad choice to become my life. I even tried to encourage my husband during one of his down moments. I explained that sometimes, we have our depressed moments. I call them my Juniper Tree experience. Depressed moments cannot turn into days. So, it was important to not allow the enemy to have long periods to keep you down. Rest if you must, but soon and very soon, you need to get up and keep it moving.

There were times that he said I was not encouraging, I was trying to turn him into me. He said I was trying to be the head of the house. No, sir! I was the head of the house when I was single, and truth be told, God has always been the head of this house (meaning my body) and every physical house that I have ever lived in or resided. He stated that he could not lead, because I would not follow. Follow where? When I asked his goals, he did not know. Then at one point, when I probed further about his passions, he listed some things, but nothing resulted in family thriving or kingdom building. It was mostly material gain. I bought dry-erase boards for the bedroom and the office. After deciding what he loved to do, there was no plan in place to achieve it. When I tried to help with that and what has worked for me, again, I was accused of trying to take charge.

I realize the enemy was choking me from my vision. I never want anyone to be like me. It's hard to be me. I don't think anyone could handle the life I have gone through, but me. I do not wish for my child to be like me. I want him to love God with his whole heart, mind, soul, and total body and love others. That is all I expect. And I know I trained him in the way he should go. What he chooses to do with that training is between him and God. I did my part as a mother. And I am grateful for the gift that God gave me with him.

Over the last few years, I have lost my vision. I mean the vision of retirement, working hard and enjoying life. I have lost the vision of keeping peace and being the glue for the family. Some family members have told me that I was the glue, but thank God, they have been there to help me stand through this storm. They have helped me remember that God is still standing by and He has never left me. I can run back to Him with open arms and He will love me just as I am.

Trust no one but God

Proverbs 3:5-6 has been a memorized scripture for most of everyone's life. We learn that scripture even before you are saved. You will notice it many times in books. On plaques, and in religious settings. It reads, "Trust in the Lord with all thine heart and lean not unto thine own understanding. In all thy ways acknowledge him, and He shall direct thy paths." During the trial of my first divorce, this scripture became true to me. I put all my trust in a person whom I shared my life with and trusted more than I trusted God. And here I am again, trusting in an imperfect vessel to provide for me, peace and security in a marriage that he has no passion for. One would think that I learned my lesson the first time. But I was like a student failing a grade. I had to repeat the test.

But this last marriage, God spoke to me through verse 7-8 of the passage. It states, "Be not wise in thine own eyes: fear the Lord, and depart from evil. It shall be health to thy navel, and marrow to thy bones." As a nurse, I know how important the umbilical cord is during pregnancy It provides nourishment to the fetus. The marrow in the bones is where red blood cells regenerate and help us to grow and maintain good posture, regeneration of new cells, and carry oxygen to the inner most parts of our body, along with the blood vessels. God is my supplier. I had to fear Him out of reverence. I could not believe everything I see. His word is my Bread and Water – everything I need to sustain a well-balanced life.

The steps to sin have not changed from the time it occurred in the Garden of Eden. The serpent started to subtly entice Eve. She repeated what Adam instructed her not to do. Yet the enemy spoke in her ear with cunning words that made her look at the fruit and draw close to evil instead of departing from it. She was not wise in her own eyes. All the time while these things were taking place, her husband was silent. He was there, because she gave it to him and he ate. The curse did not come until he consumed it. There have been discussions on who was wrong. They were both wrong. She did not submit to her husband's authority and he did not cover her with protection of God's word. The steps to sin continue to be the lust of the eye, the lust of the flesh and the pride of life. I have gotten better at trusting the Lord. I am recognizing His voice more. It is imperative that I remain healthy and continue the blood supply to my bones. I sum it up with 3 John 2, "Beloved, I wish above all things that thou mayest prosper and be in health, even as thy soul prospereth." This passage lets me know that the nourishment for my soul affects the health of my body. When I reverence God, stay in His word, worship and praise Him constantly, and obey His command, I can abide in him and He will abide in me to keep me healthy. And if the spirit of infirmity ever invades my body, I have the Balm in Gilead to heal me. The stripes He receive prior to His crucifixion was a deposit for every sickness. The hem of His garment has enough healing to make me whole. God knows, I have had to reach out many times to recover from physical, emotional, spiritual, financial and mental health issues.

So, as I revert to Proverbs 3, verses 9-10 also helped me to understand how I can ensure and seal the promise of verse 6. I know it is a matter of trust. But one way I learned to show trust is through obedience. GIVING! Want to really know if there is true love – watch the action of giving. Verse 9 does reference about honoring God with thy substance and first fruit – dealing with the tithes. I have had discussions telling me that it is not necessary to tithes because "Jesus died and because of grace, we are not under the law." I agree, it is not necessary, because God does not need our money. It all belongs to Him anyway. And yes, we are under grace. But don't be deceived. If you're are not sowing nothing, you will not reap nothing. To me, it is a command, and I will obey. Jesus stated that He did not come to do away with the law but to fulfill the law. And I may not do everything in the Bible, but the things that I know to do, I will. The word also says he that knows to do right and does not, it is sin! (paraphrased). So Old Testament or New Testament, it is still the word of God. I honor Him with my substance by helping others in need. I tithed as He has commanded. I do not want anything in the house of God to have lack, be broken, or missing because of my lack of giving or stinginess. I trust it to the Lord knowing that He will provide a Luke 6:38 blessing in my life. I trust it in the hand of God, because I know He is a way maker and a miracle worker. I have seen it in my health and finances. I have witnessed it with others and my own life.

I dare you to trust Him, even when you cannot trace Him and watch the benefits you see in your life.

Bounce Back

Remember I talked about Pastor Debra Morton's sermon "Bounce Back" spoken in 2008? I still have a bounce-back initiative. I have the power to speak a word over my life. God has brought prophets to confirm His Word. I am grateful for another chance to be healed and on the path to wholeness. This time, I will heal from the inside out. I will have full deliverance and keep my mind clear and my heart pure from the ways of the evil one. I will bounce back beyond where I was. I will not lack. Nothing will be broken or missing. Everything will work according to God's plan.

I love when Paul stated in 2 Corinthians 4:16-18, "Therefore we do not lose heart. Even though our outward man is perishing, yet the inward man is being renewed day by day. For our light affliction, which is but for a moment, is working for us a far more exceeding and eternal weight of glory, while we do not look at the things which are seen, but at the things which are not seen. For the things which are seen are temporary, but the things which are not seen are eternal." My harvest is coming. I have not planted seeds of corruption. I planted seeds that will reap good fruit. God has given me things that will sustain me throughout eternity. He has given me the Holy Spirit to help me understand the in His kingdom is goodness. And I must obey and trust Him to allow His kingdom on earth as it is in heaven. My pastor taught us that we hold the keys. But there is no sense in just holding the keys and not using them for their purpose. It is time to unlock some doors and loose the promises of God. I am excited about the future God has planned for me. I welcome every morning. I thank Him for new mercies and grace to sustain me. I am grateful for His word that is alive in me. I am grateful for the promises that He still has in store. Eye have not seen; ear hasn't heard; nor has it been revealed to my heart what the Lord has in store for me, as I walk up right in Him. As I mentioned before, there is no good thing that He will withhold from me.

Even though, I have failed at marriage, I can say that I loved with all I had, with all my heart, with all my mind, with all my body, and for that, I am grateful to know that I know how to love.

~6~

Embracing the impossible

When others say "no" – but they said in the beginning they would do anything for you or always be there when you need them. Well, so many lessons are learned on the journey of life. The word of God says to trust in the Lord with all your heart, not to put your trust in man. I know I trusted many. But when that trust is lost, it is so hard to get it back. Please don't get me wrong, there have been times when I was not trusted. I broke that trust due to infidelity with my son's dad. It did not matter that he did it first. What mattered was that I was the more spiritual one. God expected me to do the right thing. The devil was pleased that I went against the word of God, so that he could remind me that I was not in the family of faith. Hahahaha, I laugh at the outcome, because I confessed to God and my husband. I am free from the sin of adultery. I have had the opportunity to cheat, but why cheat against God? Even if no one would know in the natural, God would have a record in the spiritual. I am at a point in life that I cannot and will not cause grief to the Holy Spirit, nor will I detour from the lifetime of eternity for a moment of pleasure. That is only by His grace. My flesh does have weaknesses, but He has helped me to change my mind to know that He is able to keep me from falling. But I must want to be kept.

One of the most difficult transitions of divorce or separation is dealing with illness. It is hard when you face health issues – alone. After every marriage or right before the divorce, I have experienced some significant health challenges. It was at my worst that I leaned more on God. I have had blood disorders, cancer scares, weight loss issues, and accidents that made me realize that a companion is needed to assist during the worst of times. But God removed people and had me trust only Him during my darkest times. I am grateful that He never allowed the enemies of my past to see me at my worst, because they would have tried to push me further into darkness. I love how Jesus cleared the room when Jarius' daughter was healed. Sometimes, God knows who needs to be involved. When He is working to change the impossible, it is important to clear the room of unbelievers, nay-sayers, procrastinators, and doubters. In the medical field, before we use the defibrillator to jump start the heart or convert an irregular heartbeat, we shout "all clear" because the energy would affect anyone in contact with the patient, bed or anything touching the patient. In life, you just have to scream, "ALL CLEAR!"

Few friends yet lots of frienemies

Just as the scripture says that everyone who calls on the name of the Lord is not going to heaven. Or the song that says, "everyone talking about heaven, ain't going." Everyone who calls you friend is not your friend. As a child, my son called everyone his friend. I told him frequently, everyone is not your friend. He would reply, "but I know him or her." I would have to explain the difference in friends versus acquaintances or associates. Webster defines friend as "a person whom one knows and with whom one has a bond of <u>mutual</u> affection, typically exclusive of sexual or family relations." An acquaintance is "a person's knowledge or experience of something or a person one knows slightly, but who is not a close friend." An associate is defined as "connect (someone or something) with something else in one's mind or a partner or colleague in business or at work."

I have had many acquaintances and associates, but I have very few friends. I can tell you immediately the names of my friends. I mean there is no hesitation. It has nothing to do with where we live nor what we have. I have people, male and female that I know would be there and have been there for me through so much. We don't talk every day and sometimes, we disagree, but we communicate with love and kindness. There are times when we feel the need for each other and reach out. Many of my friends do not know each other, but they have heard of each other. Let me admit, Facebook and Instagram have nothing to do with who and how to choose friends. These are avenues on allowing people in your personal space that may cause havoc in your relationships. They are good tools when used properly, but like a gun, in the wrong hands, they can become deadly.

Lost love

The cliché of 'It is better to have loved and lost than to not love at all' is true. I think the words better or lost should be changed to say, "it hurts to have loved and lost than to not love at all" or "it is better to have loved and be filled with joy than to not love at all." I understood what the person meant, but lost love is not fun. Then I had to realize that love is never lost. You never fall out of love with a person. If people say they do, I become concerned to what they loved from the start. When you choose to stop loving a person, you make a decision not to love the actions of what they did or did not do. Because they were attached to the action, people say they don't love them anymore.

I never understood why I was told that "I just don't love you anymore." Really? According to the word of God, God is love. When you say you are a child of God, how can you not love me. Ohhhh, because you LUSTED after me or something about me. When things did not go the way you wanted, then falling out of LUST was easy.

I finally understand from the standpoint of God's word. I never stopped loving my son's dad. I never will. I know we had different values, beliefs, and thoughts for many things. But those differences allowed us to come together to produce the best gift God could have ever provided. I am still cherishing that gift today.

With my current marriage, despite our differences, I love him still. There has been some major hurt – physically, emotionally, mentally, socially, financially, and spiritually, but I love him just a much. I even long for his companionship, not to be abused, but because I believed the words he spoke to me. I trusted that he would be a man of his word. I trust God to keep me even when he could not fulfill his promises. God has done just that.

I realize the expectations I had in each marriage, but the last marriage was different because he represented God's word. He told me things that I believed he would honor because he knew God. Well, the word of God says in John 15:15, "Henceforth I call you not servants; for the servant knoweth not what his lord doeth: but I have called you friends; for all things that I have heard of my Father I have made known unto you." He could quote scripture, take me exactly where to find it, but had issues with my works for God and my past. He always asked me why I loved him, and I replied because he "knew the word." You see quoting scripture is good, living scripture is God.

Just a few contrasts:
- I was the breadwinner; he wanted to stay home
- I paid bills; he wanted to spend the money
- I love to travel and plan in advance; he was a spur-of-the-moment without vision or counting the cost

Don't misunderstand, I love adventure and surprises, but you must plan. How can two walk together unless they agree? It is difficult. There will always be stress and strife in the relationship. Boundaries must be set. We failed to set boundaries. NOW, the relationship is lost.

Raising a child to be a man – alone

As a single mom, I thank God for the grace to raise such a handsome and wise young man. I have heard people say that a single mom cannot teach a boy how to be a man. That is true, but I know God said that He would be everything that we need. When my son was growing up, God provided so much male attention from my father, my father-in-love, brothers, church deacons, military and community friends. My son went to professional sporting events, attending fishing trips, was taught and played every sport. He had a village of men from different races, religions, ethnic groups and nationalities to care for and love on him. Even now, friends call to ask how he is doing. He never wanted for anything.

The men I married attempted to remove him from my life. There was always a jealous spirit in my relationships. One husband told me that his mom never treated him like I treat my son. My response, "I am not your mother." I was even told by one that if I give up my son, our marriage would work. I know nothing comes before your marriage, but when an insecure man cannot differentiate the love of a mother for her son from the love of a wife for her husband, there is a major problem anyway. Why should I give up a gift that God gave to me for a relationship that is based on conditions of what I will do? In addition to that, I was not able to have more children, but a man was always standing by waiting for a chance.

To any woman that has been force or is asked to make a choice between your child and your husband (when your child is in the developmental years and is not running your house), it's time to reevaluate your marriage. Check the selfishness of your spouse. Then people wonder why black men are not loving their families…. because, they do not know how. They (not all men) have become so insecure that they become jealous of their own children. I may be alone, but I am not lonely. Praise God for that.

When passion is gone

As I return to complete the book, I had a call from my husband to tell me he wanted a divorce. I thought I was strong enough to handle when this day comes. I expected it. I prepared for it. We had been separated three times and this last time, for over a year. But I had hope that God would restore and work this marriage so that others could see that God is a God of impossibilities. But the things he said to me were like a hot knife penetrating my heart. Even when I tried to speak kindly and still apologize for my wrongs or perceived wrongs, he found a way to make me feel like I was lower than a piece of crap in the toilet. He said, "I should have done this years ago and I am ready to move forward with this decision." What?!! I was the one abused. I was the one manipulated and thought there was hope.

But as I review the scenes of previous events, he told me over four years ago, "the Holy Spirit told me that there was nothing left in this marriage." Well, why did he not listen to the Holy Spirit and get out then? He kept returning for sex, money, blocking opportunities for me to advance. And then walking away when it was convenient for him. When he wasn't working, I did everything. When he found a job, he would find an excuse to leave, so he did not have to help me pay bills. I still have trouble figuring that out.

On one occasion he stated, "I don't feel passion when we kiss." Lord, what was I to do? How can I please his every desire and take care of home? Sex was not paying the bills. I could not just lay around all day in the bed ready with my legs spread to please him. At times, I wish I could, but in reality, it was not possible. We were not millionaires, nor were millions on the horizon to come in. I wish I would have known that my spouse chose another woman over me! I would have ended it, too. But I did not know. I was hoping against all odds.

Well, ... loyalty means everything in a marriage! But when the enemy is invited in, the door is left open and your covering chooses to walk away or spread malicious lies!! Then you realize this is not new! He has been plotting this for a while. Surely, he did not just wake up one morning and decide to just walk away and give up such a wonderful life.

No matter what occurs in your marriage, good or bad, right or wrong.... Don't allow your friends or your family to get between you & your spouse. Don't associate with anyone who hates, disrespects & dishonors your spouse. Make them clearly understand that you & your spouse are one. Anyone who truly cares about you will honor your choice of spouse & will treat your spouse with dignity & respect. Anyone who comes to you to gossip about your spouse is sowing seeds of division in your marriage; stop them immediately. Shield your marriage. Protect your spouse's position, image & reputation. Stand up in defense for each other. "What God has joined together, let no one separate." Mark 10:9. ♡ ♡ It is terrible when your spouse is causing the separation. It is even worse, when your spouse is saying disparaging things to your family and his. God sees all and hears all.

I still did not clearly understand how the passion or lack of passion was from me. He made me feel as though I was the problem. I believed it. I was the issue. I did everything I could to prove to him that I was passionate. I am a romantic. I love and enjoy pleasing my man. I even was willing to do things that he preferred, BUT

God did not allow it to happen. I bought sex toys. I even took him shopping in a sex store to pick out what he thought would help. That ecstasy lasted for a month. Then I was interrogated: Who I was using the toys on? Why were they moved from previous places? (even though some were kept in a drawer with other hair-care products). They were doomed to be moved at times. The sexual connection was not the issue, it was the control he wanted to have over me to dictate.

I finally understand that passion he alluded to is an Eros type love that he had for me. When you love someone with AGAPE love that God requires, you will have the joy and peace within the relationship that takes you from day to day and gets your through trials and tribulations. That type of love leaves a passion to cause you to come home through hell and high water to please your man. The type of love that causes you to stay close to home to help encourage your man to be the best that he can be. The type of love to plan things to help him keep his mind off day-to-day issues that lowers his self-esteem. The type of love to never bring up financial issues or health issues that could cause him to worry. The type of love that chooses not to expose all the terrible things done to discredit me, while forgiving the things that hurt me. The type of love that would put his needs first. The type of love to never boast about what I have, but to understand that we have it together and pray that if things were different I could be assured that he would do the same for me.

When passion is gone from the other person, it can only be resurrected, if they want it to be. When you try and he or she continues to look for the worse or expects the worse to happen, you're fighting an uphill battle. But that is the time to look to the hills from where your help comes from. Your help comes from God. Trust in Him to restore whatever needs to be restored in your life.

Always remember: Whatever the head does, the body follows. A sermon Bishop T.D. Jakes preached one Sunday that blessed me was "Get Your Head Right." We cannot live by the heart. We must be strong enough to lead and live with our minds and the results will flow into the heart. If it is of God, it will work. If it is against God's Word, there will be consequences.

To Sacred Peace...

~7~

Get Pass Your Past

Seven is stated to be the number of perfection. We have been married legally for seven years (while I was writing this book). Out of the seven years, we have lived together almost three. It's so weird, I am at peace and keep praying for reconciliation and restoration. Some people tell me that I should just keep holding on and wait for God to turn things around. Some tell me that because of his decision, God has already answered my prayer and He has someone better for me. I am content in the state I am in...with God.

Assess/examine yourself

So, let's assess the situation. Assessments work in any area of your life. This works in the arena of medical practice and it will work in everyday life. A great example: the flu. There are signs of the flu – feeling bad, unable to move, no appetite, sluggish, tired, etc. There are symptoms of the flu – fever, achy muscles, sneezing, coughing, stuffy head, difficulty breathing, etc. The key to flu, it can incubate in the body for days without signs and symptoms, but once it presents itself, it can start to resolve by day 3, but the worst of the symptoms can linger for up to seven days. Another thing about the flu, it is a virus and has to take its course. You can treat the symptoms, but they will still present themselves. The best thing to do is rest, force fluids and allow it to take its course. The trauma arises when other bacteria and illnesses attack while the virus has invaded.

When you assess or examine your life, you must gather information. Whether it is physical, mental, emotional, social, financial, or spiritual, gather the information and assess the situation. This is something that should take just a few minutes. Just brainstorm the issue. What is going on? List all the issues, good, bad, and ugly – an overall snapshot of the situation. For example – decreased finances, infidelity in the marriage, abuse, rejection, job issues, church hurt, pain, illnesses, disease, mental instability, memory lapses, etc.

What are the signs presented in situation? Inability to meet your monthly budget or bills? Not enough income? Increased lies and dishonesty? Increased accusations? Feelings of jealousy? Increased complaining? Lack of passion in the marriage/relationship? Disloyalty? Lack of responsibility? Hiding things? Secret conversations? Inability to stay on task? Changes in normal routines that led to success? Procrastination? Low self-esteem? Hopelessness? Just cannot understand? What can you see going on? This is the ability to do objective or observing what you see is wrong. Sometimes, people see things before you recognize them. Part of assessing is recognizing what you see. What is spoken or perceived from people involved? This is the part of the assessment that is told to you. When a doctor or medical person walks in the exam room, he/she is trained to visualize you from head to toe to get a snapshot as to what is wrong. Back to the flu case – when he/she enters the room and notice you covered, it is suspected that you have chills and fever. Usually, the higher the fever the more you have chills because the body is attempting to compensate to cool you. And the red-flushed look shows the heat that your body is exhibiting, or paleness shows that you are dehydrated and need fluids, while a blueness to the skin or mucus membranes portray lack of oxygen and there are major symptoms/problems presenting. Then he/she starts to ask questions – what brought you in today? How long has it been going on? What did you take to alleviate the problem? Whatever you tell the doctor is subjective information to help develop a diagnosis and plan to eliminate the problem.

What symptoms are presented? Unable to contribute financially to the normal routine bills. Lack of paying tithes and offering? Utilities turned off? Asking for funds to pay bills? Repossessions? Spreading rumors about your spouse? Manipulating others for information? Lying about past issues? Flirting in public? People of opposite sex over-friendly/disrespectful? Feelings of insecurity? Aggressiveness in public? Quoting scripture for their gain? Social media excessiveness or hiding? There are so many things that one must be aware of to have a flourishing relationship.

Diagnose the Issue

Gather all the information and come to a conclusion of what the root of the problem is. When a doctor suspects flu, he/she orders tests specific to the illness. There are other tests that are run for another illness, pneumonia. Flu and pneumonia present the same and have the same signs and symptoms, but the treatments are different. Remember, flu is caused by a virus. Pneumonia is caused by bacteria. Bacteria is treated with antibiotics. A virus has to take its course and symptoms are treated. Once the bacteria is treated, the symptoms go away. So, it is important to get to the right diagnosis, in order to provide the correct treatment. Pneumonia and heart failure present the same, but one test differentiates the two. With pneumonia the treatment is to force fluids and use antibiotics. With heart failure, fluids are limited because too much can cause the heart to stop. The diagnosis or the root of the issue is important.

To understand brokenness, one must get to the root of the problem. You must uncover the issues and understand how they started. The initial start could be a generational curse or just some way the enemy sees the weakness and continues to use that particular area in your life.

In my case, marriage has been my issue, but the root of the problem may be from the child molestation or sexual assaults, which can cause ungodly spirits of jealousy, whoredom, fear, error, divination, heaviness, haughtiness, and anti-Christ. Even though I have been delivered from my past, the enemy still does his job well to try and remind us of our wrong. When I chose to share with my spouse before we were married, he initially told me it did not matter. I felt that I could trust him with my life. But later, he looked at it as I was unclean. He took what I shared with him in confidence, to our pastor. He made it seem like, I could not be trusted. Yet I had to understand that he had his own demons and strongholds that he faced. Instead of dealing with his issues, he chose to suppress his past and resurface mine by reading a diary that I kept years before we met, and to expose my past in the church. But what he meant for evil, God worked it out for good. God already had plans for the book, <u>The Woman at the Well: From Guilt to Grace</u>. He catapulted it to be published. Little did he know that the enemy was attempting to stop me with my past, but God was building me up for my future! Choose ye this day whom you will serve.

I know I am delivered. I know that I am forgiven for my past, because now I can talk about the issues and use my past to help others. The future God has in store will be a legacy that others can use for growth and elimination of shame. I am not boasting in my past, but I am boasting in the God, Who has through His grace and mercy allowed me to get pass my past. I have learned to depend on Jesus. He is my Friend. He is my Guide. I learn how to lean on Him in good times and to depend on Him to carry me in the tough times. It is when I take my eyes off Him, I lose my way.

I fell in love and prayed to walk together with a man that could quote scripture, tell me where to find it within seconds, and pray like he sits at the right hand of God. But I never took time to watch the fruit that should have been produced. There is a difference in falling on hard times versus contributing to hard times out of greed and selfishness.

Before you entertain someone for potential long-term relationship, count the cost, understand who they are and what they have gone through, and try the spirit to make sure it is of God. That is the best way to diagnose any issues. Use 1 John 4:1 as a guideline to help you obtain the best diagnosis.

Plan for the best

Remember Jeremiah 29:11 says God knows the plans that He has for me and it is to have hope and a future. I also love Proverbs 16:3 that tells me to commit my ways to the Lord, and they will succeed (paraphrased). The King James Version says, "Commit they works unto the Lord, and thy thoughts shall be established." In other words, He will help me develop the best plan of action, according to His will.

From a medical standpoint, once the diagnosis is made, a plan of action is started. The plan of action includes everything and everyone necessary to get the best prognosis or cure. The goal is always to get the patient back to the state of functioning prior to the illness or to a point of optimum ability.

If you notice when you walk into an emergency department, you are met at the desk for initial intake of information, then you are triaged by a tech or nurse to obtain history, vital signs and reason for coming. Depending on your severity, you will be seen sooner if you have chest pain, stroke, breathing issues, or profuse bleeding or massive trauma compared to cold or minor issues that could be taken care of in a doctor's office. Later you are moved to a room and asked more questions to obtain more detailed information. Then the tests begin to come to a more definitive diagnosis. Lab techs, radiology techs, ultra sound techs, nurses, practitioners, administrative techs, and physicians all work together to provide the best care that leads to best prognosis. Notice you are even asked about insurance. That's another book. It is important to have your ability to pay and plan for future issues that may arise. This is flagged in their system.

What about in a relationship or marriage? We as women can cause damage to ourselves and our man by not allowing him to be the man or provider. There is a difference when he never planned to be. It should not take anyone 5 years to find some source of income to take care of his family or to contribute to the better outcome of the family.

When the only plan you have is to take from the relationship and only contribute good sex, there will be damage. I am a witness, that eventually, he will get tired of you and want someone else. Or you will become disabled financially and he will leave because the well has gone dry. He was in search of finding women who could do more for him. It is difficult to have champagne taste on a beer budget or wino-sharing mentality. What do I mean by "wino-sharing"? My brothers use to talk about certain guys in the community that would drink "just" brand. I asked what is "just" brand? The explanation – Just whatever you provide, they will drink, and they never contributed to the funds or the stash.

I set myself up for damage. When we married, I was set financially with a 401K, stock plan, mutual funds, a house, a few checking and saving accounts, at different banks and credit unions, medical and life insurance, as well as a will. I shared all of this with him. He was without a job, a car, rented a town house (that I paid the last three month's rent), child support arrears that was years behind for two different children, no type of insurance nor future plans for saving anything. What he had,...a word from the Lord and a plan to manipulate his way through. I bought into it, not completely, but enough that I sold myself for his way.

I thought we could plan and start a business together as we worked in ministry to help the community. But my plans were not his plans. His ways were not my ways. He was unemployed, and I thought helping to start a business would be something that he would do while I was away working to have stable income, until we had enough for me to start working the business together. When we were together, I helped to encourage him, but sometimes, I was too hard (according to him). But when you invest in something, you must work it to yield a good return. We had a good plan in place. We even prayed about some things together, but after a few weeks, it was not what he wanted. He enjoyed sleeping in late and going to bed early and taking a nap during the day.

He did not mind robbing Peter to pay Paul. He always had excuses of why it could not be done, rather than doing whatever necessary to excel. I bought in to the lies and excuses. I worked more. I brought in more money. I never allowed the house to go without, until he told me that he was not there to take care of me. Lord, help me!!!

Implement and take action

A plan is ineffective unless there are actions involved. The slogan used many years ago, "a failure to plan is a plan to fail." This holds true. Yet it is even more detrimental to life to have a plan and never follow it. Faith without works is dead. I sat in a seminar in 2016 and the presenter stated, "What moves God is action! Faith requires action. Faith without works is dead." Some people pray and expect God to do the work. I ask God to strengthen me to do what needs to be done and take charge when I cannot move forward. He provides and equips us to do what is necessary, as He is with us and works through us. He does supernatural things to help us reach the finish product.

I remember a well renown pastor stating in a sermon, "the richest place on earth is the cemetery." After listening intently, I realized that it is true, because in the ground lies ideas that were never birthed. Plans that were never fulfilled. Obstacles that were never faced or confronted. Lives that were never lived in abundance. I do not want to leave this earth without seeing all of God's promises fulfilled in my life. God knows that I have attempted to give up, pass out, quit and throw in the towel during my journey. But because of His power that works in me, I cannot. I will not. I shall not. I must move on in faith, by His grace and with His mercies.

There were many times that I did not have faith to go to work. I felt like a failure. I felt the evil things working on me. I stopped being organized. I started to procrastinate. I stopped counting the cost and planning. I started believing the bad things that were being said about me. Maybe I was too hard. Maybe I was attempting to turn him into me. Maybe I was putting too much of my traits in his children to take away his identity. That was never my intention. I want to help others be a success. According to the word of God, it is my duty to encourage and be a blessing to others, especially my family. But the plans I had did not work.

Reassess

It's ok to change the plan but keep your eye on the goal. I allowed my plans to suffer and almost lost everything. I moved to Louisiana out of shame because of the abuse. I needed to get away. I realized that God had a plan that was bigger than mine. I continued to save and received great dividends from work. I moved back to my home in Texas because once again, I was ashamed of the state of the marriage. I did not want to face people we knew. I was embarrassed because I allowed so much to happen that was not righteous. I caused some and I consented to some.

Where was my faith? Where was my trust? And if I had trust, who was my trust in? When the day of judgement comes, who will I answer to? I had to remember my Source. I tried to find out where I went wrong. To be honest, I went wrong even before the marriage started. I knew he was not for me. Even though he has his side of the story to tell, I know what he brought the table.... NOTHING!!! My church life changed. My family life changed. My work life changed. My personal life changed. All for the worse and I tried to hold on to someone whose job was to take me off course from what God was doing in my life. It worked! BUT only for a little while!

Remember the bounce-back discussion. When you reassess, you review everything that was done. What worked? What did not work? How did it affect the outcome or goal? Is there a better way or quicker response to improve the end result? Did you really count the cost? Cling to what is good. Stand fast on God's principles. Know that He fights for you. Command the angels to go to work on your behalf. Speak His words so that heaven will move for you. And when you reassess and revitalize, keep your eyes on the prize. Know that the joy of the Lord is your strength. There is no good thing that He will withhold from you if you walk upright in Him. And during the time of reassessing, clear the room. Get quiet before the Lord and listen to what He tells you. Then do what He designed for your to do.

~8~

Restore versus Refurbish

Puzzles

When working with a sales company, the research lab would take old pieces and use them for some new models. We would ask customers if they preferred a new model or a refurbished model. With refurbished parts, the guarantee or life of the part was older than the actual machine. The rationale: if the part fits and functions, then it was good to go.

Life cannot be refurbished. We are restored. We go through issues that seem to take us off track. While taking time to recuperate, we are restored to usefulness. When people come to the hospital we assess their problems and attempt to restore them to their optimal health.

People are like a puzzle. You take your life plans, goals, experiences, hopes, and dreams, put them together to make a beautiful portrait of your life. When you die, they develop your obituary to give the congregation a snapshot of the final picture of your life. You cannot fit the entire lifespan on paper, but enough is written to show the life of the person and the loved ones they left. Sometimes it is hard to visualize the life of someone in such a short moment. When you know them, it is easier to put it all together.

Putting the pieces together

I always loved doing puzzles. I enjoyed the 500 or more pieces. It was therapeutic for the brain. You always started with the smooth edges and corners. The challenge for me was not always putting it together but developing a strategy to put it together quicker. Finding all the edges was sometimes mind-boggling. Your eyes were crossed at the end of the day. Sometimes, I would have to walk away and return later to have a fresh start.

It's the same in marriage. Find the smooth edges of things that a person likes and understand how those pieces fit together to make the borders of the relationship. We must set boundaries. What works for me may not always work for my husband. When we first married, I prayed kneeling at night before getting in bed and when I work up early in the morning. He told me that was not necessary. Well, maybe not for him. But it was for me. That was my smooth edge to keep me surrounded by the presence of God.

He would try to make me sleep in on Saturday. I just could not sleep past 7am. But I made it a point not to disturb him when I woke up. I cooked breakfast on Saturday, just as my mom and grandma. They always felt that when a person could smell breakfast, it was time to get up. Well, many times, I cooked and ate, while he and his children slept until 11am or sometimes, afternoon. But I never complained. I just knew that we had different boundaries.

Jagged edges

Notice that puzzle pieces come with jagged edges. If all the edges were smooth, it would not be a challenge to put it together. No two pieces are the same shape, nor do they have the same picture. Some pieces are very closely related, but not the same. The same in marriage, no two people are alike. My husband would often tell me that we were alike. I did not see it. Yes, we liked some of the same things, but we were so different that it cost us our marriage due to disloyalty.

Marriage is work. Sometimes, you may have to walk away to get some clarity, not to have an affair. Even the Bible asks how can two walk together, unless they agree? It also says that we should not defraud ye not one the other, except it be with consent for a time, that ye may give yourselves to fasting and prayer; and come together again that satan tempt you not for your inconsistency.

I guess our problem was not with stepping away, but more of consenting to step away or separate. When I needed time away, he never consented and told me God would not bless me. When he wanted to leave, he would cause a major argument and then leave. I took my time allowing him to come back. Both were wrong approaches from people professing to be Christians. We will each pay the penalty for the sin we committed not to keep the marriage together.

Getting it all back

I realized that sometimes you must lose in order to winTo move up higher, you must have a sturdy foundation. In learning architect, I understood that the higher the building, the deeper the foundation. The word of God says that when we are faithful over little, He will make us ruler over much.

I look forward to the destiny God has for me. I am grateful that I am not defeated. I will continue to love like I have never loved before. I enjoy companionship. I do not and will not allow abuse or mistreatment in any way to me nor my family. I do not want to return to any part of my past. I am beyond that time. I look forward to what God will be doing. He is a Rewarder of those that diligently seek Him. I am seeking Him. I am hungering and thirsting after His word. I know that my harvest is great. I have been gleaning in the wrong field.

It's restoration time. I no longer expect things to happen. I make things happen. If anyone desires to bless me, I am grateful. I will not sit around and wait for no one to treat me better than God treats me. It will not happen. Only He can provide the environment needed for me to have a blessed, fruitful marriage. I am a wife, a good one. Whoever finds me (by the standards of

God) will have a good thing and will be favored of the Lord. One of my favorite scriptures is Proverbs 14:1. I thank God for the ability to have wisdom to build a home. Until the appointed time, I will rest and wait as discussed in Isaiah 40:31. Waiting on the Lord means that I am working, watching, and worshipping. I am not sitting idly by waiting for anyone to take care of me. I messed up numerous times taking care of a man. So much to a point of him not wanting to take care of anything. I was prey. At times, I opened the door for the enemy to come in and take over my life. A place that only God has the right to own.

Baby steps to giant leap

You have to crawl before your walk. Do not spend all your time crawling through life waiting for things to happen. Sometimes, you have to run and take a leap of faith. There is nothing new under the sun. Find someone who has done it and succeeded at it, then follow their processes. Reassess the process and make sure it takes you to the desired destiny. No more U-turns or detours, unless there are dangers ahead. Remember: Proverbs 3:5-6 "trust in the Lord with all your heart and lean not to your own understanding. In all your ways acknowledge Him and He will direct your path."

From my Facebook page, I posted this in 2015 after our cruise. Sometimes, God would send messages by way of social media. At the time when I was going through a depressed moment, this helped me to start my bounce back moment.

My end of the year MOTIVATION gift to someone:

You aren't the only one who made mistakes this year. You aren't the only one who failed, messed up, struggled, missed the mark, and lost some battles. You aren't the only one who cried because of the disappointments, discouragement, defeat, delay and dismissals. You aren't the only one who lost love, lost friendships, lost a job, lost clients, missed opportunities, missed chances and missed moments. You aren't the only one who had to keep your secret safe behind your smile. You aren't the only one who feels empty. This is life. ** Everybody's got a problem they're dealing with in SILENCE hidden behind a SMILE. ** But regardless of what it seems like, the GREATEST GIFT of LIFE is LIFE ITSELF. The ability to breathe again, try again, work again, love again, laugh again, smile again. Tomorrow you get a second chance. You aren't the only one to NEED a SECOND chance. So, hold your head high. You still have a chance. NEW opportunities, NEW relationships, NEW miracles and NEW blessings. So, cry! It's okay. You aren't the only one! Hurt! It's okay. You aren't the only one! Laugh! It's okay. You aren't the only one! Because everything is going to be okay. YOU are going to HAVE better and LIVE better. Because you are the only YOU in the WORLD. And no matter what went right or wrong this year, YOUR LIFE is NOT and will NEVER be a mistake. Get ready for your second chance. You aren't the only one who needs one!

New wine in old wineskin

According to biblical times, when you put new wine in old wineskin, the container would burst and cause you to lose all the contents. There comes a time when we must change the inside and the outside as well. So many reality shows call change "a complete or extreme makeover." Eventually, when the Holy Spirit takes over, there will be a change in the outward appearance. But I have learned that what worked for my grandma may not work for me in this day and time. We must be open to new things, new thoughts, new ways of doing things. That does not mean that we become disobedient; we need to be transformed by the renewing of our mind. We cannot keep doing things the same way expecting different results.

I learn great relationship techniques from my nieces and nephews, as well as my son and some of his friends. They can give me insight on red flags that I may not see in a person. They keep me focused on my value and how important I am, while I help to relate it in the spiritual realm.

In the last marriage, I was prepared to be the breadwinner, but only for a little while. I learned that when you are good to some people, they continue to expect goodness without contributing to make it better. As long as you are giving to them without expectation, they will keep taking. I have never had a bank account that was empty, and the teller allowed me to withdraw funds. You must put something in to get something out. A relationship without love deposits will leave the giver worn out, depressed, unfulfilled, hopeless, and lonely. Rupture leads to excessive loss. Once there is rupture, it is hard to repair.

~9~

Sacred peace found in God

Restoration

Everything has it's season. And one of the great signs of faith is learning to accept when things have come to an end. Recently we've been hearing that a lot of people are struggling to let go of certain relationships even though they know those relationships are no longer productive. Today you need to affirm the fact that God wants you to live a purposeful and productive life. Strive to live your on purpose even if that means cutting ties with people who you've grown accustomed to having around. The Bible says in Ecclesiastes 3:2-3 that there is, "a time to plant and a time to uproot, a time to kill and a time to heal, a time to tear down and a time to build." Just because a relationship was good in the past doesn't mean it needs to have a place in your future. After the planting season comes the season of uprooting and both are necessary. Because if you never uproot you will be sitting around a bunch of dying plants. Choose life instead.

Never give up

Open those curtains. Spread back the drapes to allow the light to come in. Get ready for the territory to be enlarged. Make preparation. I heard Pastor John Gray say in a sermon recently, as a matter of fact, it was a few hours after crying when my husband said he wanted a divorce. He stated, "If you are still holding on to the promise that God gave you, don't give up! It's your turn. You have worked consistently and prayed. Get ready! You're next! God has not forgotten about you. He sees all that you have gone through. He sees how faithful you have been. It's your turn! He moved people out of your way. He eliminated those that He knew would not help you to reach your destiny. It's your turn!" People of God, don't grow weary in well doing. The harvest is coming. Sometimes, we plant seeds and move to another area looking for a harvest. Only to find that we were planting seeds in the wrong garden. What is even worse, sometimes, we don't really plant, we just scatter, and this leads to weeds and other deadly, non-fruitful plants growing in what could be a beautiful garden. I cannot and will not give up on God.

Shame has caused me to isolate myself and play into the enemy's trap! Thank God for prayer warriors that don't just pray, they act! I AM not my many marriages or divorces. I AM not the molestation from my childhood. I AM not the rape victim from the past. I AM not the disappointments or lack of achievements that society has placed on me! I AM not my doubts and fears! I AM not a religion, color, size, or shape! I AM naked, but not ashamed! I have taken off the old clothes and put on the new! I have been filled with good fruit, Godly fruit that will live throughout eternity! I AM REDEEMED! I AM a Godly woman filled with the Holy Spirit that causes me to love, live, and encourage!!! I AM the product of a risen Savior that gave His life so that I may live, not just to get by, but live abundantly. I AM a believer destined for heaven. I WILL glorify my Father in all I do, because it is through His grace that my broken, beat-up body is strong enough to continue this journey!

Faith

I talked a little of about faith earlier. And I cannot stress enough how important faith is to life. It is like oxygen is to air; air is to the body; the body is to life; and life is to the Spirit. It takes faith to live from day to day. The word of God says that everyone has been given a measure of faith. We all have it, whether we know it or not. The key is: do you believe it, and will you exercise it? Jesus told His disciples it is with mustard seed faith that mountains can be removed.

I understand so much more of God's word at this point in my life, and I have so much more to learn. I have faith to know that I will not walk this journey alone. When I was in the military stationed in Texas, my pastor told me that God was going to bless me with a love from a husband to bless me and provide all that I need to enjoy my life as a wife and mother. He has gone on to be with the Lord, but I still hold to that word that he spoke. He told me that I have so much love to give and it cannot just be given to any man. But my job is to trust and obey God's word and believe that he is faithful to do what He said, as I am faithful to do what I need to do for Him.

According to Hebrews 11:1, it is a "Now faith!" Not yesterday's faith or grandma's faith. Not your spouse's faith. It is a NOW faith that helps us through life's trials. I refuse to hang between the two thieves of yesterday and tomorrow. Yesterday is not coming back and tomorrow is not promised. I walk in the promises that God has stored up for me. He has given me access to kingdom living and by faith, I will enjoy heaven here on earth. I am like David, I am convinced. Like Paul, I am confident. Like Joshua, I am courageous. Like Moses, I am strong. Like Abraham, I am trusting. Like Timothy, I am teachable. Like my grandma, I am hopeful! He is a God of promise. I may not see the promise yet. I may not understand how the promise will happen. But I know He is faithful and just to forgive and cleanse me, as He is preparing me for greater. Until the promise is fulfilled, I will hope in His word. Not in my ability, because that can change. Not in my beauty, because they can fade away. Not in my income, because that goes so fast. Not in my title, because I really do not profit anything. Only my faith in Him is what guides me daily.

Promises

The Bible is filled with more than 3,000 promises, some are automatic, and some are with certain actions to activate the promise. Just a few of my favorites that has helped me throughout the years:

Ephesians 3:20 - Now unto Him that is able to do exceeding abundantly above all that we ask or think, according to the power that works in us.

Exodus 20:12 – Honour thy father and thy mother: that thy days may be long upon the land which the Lord thy God giveth thee.

Psalm 90:10 – The days of our years are threescore years and ten: and if by reason of strength they be fourscore years, yet is their strength labour and sorrow; for it is soon cut off, and we fly away.

Psalm 91:16 – With long life will I satisfy him, and shew him my salvation.

Matthew 6:33 – But seek ye first the kingdom of God, and His righteousness; and all these things shall be added unto you.

John 15:7 – If ye abide in Me, and my words abide in you, ye shall ask what ye will, and it shall be done unto you.

Matthew 7:7-8 – ask, and it shall be given you; seek, and ye shall find; knock, and it shall be open unto you:

for everyone that asketh receiveth; and he that seeketh findeth: and to him that knocketh it shall be opened.

Luke 6:38 – Give, and it shall be given unto you; good, measure, pressed down, and shaken together, and running over, shall men give into your bosom, for with the same measure that ye mete withal it shall be measured to you again.

Galatians 6:7 – Be not deceived; God is not mocked: for whatsoever a man soweth, that shall he also reap.

Galatians 6:9 – And let us not be weary in well doing; for in due season we shall reap, if we faint not.

Isaiah 26:3 – Thou wilt keep him in perfect peace, Whose mind is stayed on Thee: Because he trusteth in thee.

1 John 1:9 – If we confess our sins, He is faithful and just to forgive us our sins, and to cleanse us from all unrighteousness.

Philippians 4:19 – But my God shall supply all your need according to His riches in glory by Christ Jesus.

Philippians 4:13 – I can do all things through Christ which strengtheneth me.

2 Chronicles 7:14 – If my people, which are called by my name, shall humble themselves, and pray, and seek my face, and turn from their wicked ways; then will I hear

from heaven, and will forgive their sin, and will heal their land.

Proverbs 16:3 – Commit they works unto the Lord, and thy thoughts shall be established.

Others include but are not conclusive: Matthew 5; Psalm 23, Psalm 1, Ephesians 6, Romans 5 & Romans 8, The story of Job gives great analogy of God's faithfulness and trust towards us and how He rewards us for our faithfulness and trust in Him.

There are so many promises, I could write a book on just His promises. As a matter of fact, it has already been done. There are many books written to guide us to what we need and what God promises to help us in time of need. He is a healer, a deliverer, a doctor, a lawyer, a giver, a provider, a shelter. He is everything we need. We must have a hunger and a thirst for His word. His word is a lamp unto my feet and a light unto my path. His word can keep me from stumbling. There should not be any darkness to cause me to trip, stumble, nor fall in life's challenges. He is directing my path to keep me on the straight and narrow.

Thirst only for righteousness

As the modern day 'woman at the well,' my thirst has been quenched. I thirst for the word of God and strive daily to be a better person. The enemy attempts to beat me down and say all the things that happen in my life are because of some wrong I have done. But the word of God tells me differently.

Matthew 5:6 says, "Blessed are they which do hunger and thirst after righteousness: for they shall be filled."

Proverbs 21:21 says, "he that followeth after righteousness and mercy findeth life, righteousness, and honor.

Isaiah 32:17 says, "And the work of righteousness shall be peace; and the effect of righteousness quietness and assurance forever.

As stated earlier, I have a long way to go and more to learn. But I have more days behind me than I do ahead of me. I will make the most of every moment He allows me to have. I am grateful for the lessons learned. I am more grateful that the enemy has no power over me to take control. I belong to God. There is not a day that goes by that I do not thank Him for saving a sinner like me. He uses me according to His plan and I am reaping a harvest that He promised.

Because of my steadfastness and obedience, He spared me. Sometimes, we must lose what we thought was best, to get the best that He has for us. I am so grateful for God's presence in my life. I love His word. I look forward to attending church. I welcome encouraging others. I love people. I understand life can be difficult, but these are just light afflictions compared to the glory God has for us. My objective everyday is to honor, obey, and seek Him first in everything I do. I once was young and now I am older, and I have never seen the righteous forsaken, nor his seed begging bread.

Keep God First

One of my favorite scriptures that often is misquoted is Matthew 6:33. It states to "But seek ye first the kingdom of God, and His righteousness; and all these things shall be added unto you." Another one is Jeremiah 29:11 which states, "For I know the plans that I have for you. They are to have hope and a future." I love so many scriptures from the word of God, because it is my way of listening to Him. He gives me the answer to questions and He provides everything that I need to make it from day to day in life.

Even though, I stated that I may never know what it will be like to be married for 50 years, I trust God enough to wait for Him to bring me His best. My age does not matter. But my heart anticipates the companionship and love that I have desired in a marriage all my life.

I understand that God delays sudden blessings because of lack trust! During my delay, it is a season to strengthen my faith! It is a season to sift my motives! God does not delay or deny because He does not love me, but more to ensure that I am prepared to receive the blessing. There is nothing worst than receiving the answer to my prayer or a blessing, only to find that I cannot maintain the blessing. God wants to ensure that

I am ready for His best. I cannot be impatient, nervous, or complain. I must wait with patience and work while I wait. I found the passage below in a devotion and wrote them in a Bible years ago.

How to wait for God:
Patiently ~~~~~~~~~~~~~~~~~~~~~~Psalm 67
Quietly ~~~~~~~~~~~~~~~~~~~~~~~Psalm 62
Trustingly ~~~~~~~~~~~~~~~~~~~~~Psalm 143
Expectantly ~~~~~~~~~~~~~~~~~~~~Psalm 27
Steadfastly ~~~~~~~~~~~~~~~~~~~~Psalm 27:14
Standing on God's Word ~~~~~~~~Psalm 130

This was a story that I found on the internet. I seem to find things at times that would help provide clues to understand my husband. Maybe it was my hope that I would find evidence to the problem to know how to deal with it. It's hard to fight for something or someone that you really don't understand. But I had to remember, that I wrestle (fight) against wickedness, power, principalities and not the flesh and blood.

Written from a broken husband:

"I don't know how to love you. That's the honest to God truth. Despite the mask that I wore when we married...my lack of attentiveness and compassion should be proof. The truth is that I am lost, stuck in this vacuum of hopeless insecurities. My desire to protect myself from the exposure of what I can't do for you drives me to hide my vulnerabilities. I never saw my dad love my mom, so my model is a figment of a false reality. I became a man before I was a boy so the undeveloped boy is reflected in the man's face that you now see. What you want, I can't provide...what you need I now don't possess...but I need you to understand that there is love but it is hidden in this heart buried inside my chest. I am afraid to be vulnerable...to me, that goes against what it means to be a man. But something inside of me is crying out for help...but this internal conflict keeps me from extending my hand. If you could see what I see when I look at me you would know how I feel. If you could hear the rhythm of my heart beat, you would know that this song of fear is real. I hate to cause you pain, it breaks my heart to see you cry. But if my broken heart breaks a little more, is that truly a reason to try? I have no one to turn to, no one to truly trust with the contents of my heart. Can you understand where I am at without taking this personal? If so, maybe this is a safe place to start..."

Your husband is crying out for help...but you may not be able to hear his heart because he is not speaking in a way that you can understand. What if you could understand him? What if you could interpret his pleas for help correctly so that you could meet him where he is? If this is you, this book was written with you in mind: www.unmotivated2love.com

Found on Pinterest in an article:

15 Things to ask in your next relationship... (no, don't limit the questions to 15, keep asking questions)

1. Do you believe in monogamy?

2. Have you ever cheated or been cheated on?

3. Have you ever been in love? What was it about that relationship or that person that made you know that it was love?

4. How does someone show you that they love you? Are you familiar with the book The 5 Love Languages ? What's your love language?

5. Has your heart ever been broken? What happened?

6. Have you ever had unprotected sex?

7. Have you been tested for STDs, including HIV? What were the results? Are you willing to get tested again?

8. Have you ever gotten into a physical altercation with a female? What were the events which led up to the altercation?

9. Why did you and your ex break-up (or divorce)? If that reason was no longer an obstacle would you be together?

10. What would your ex(es) say about you and the circumstances surrounding your breakup?

11. Are you friends with your ex? Do you still communicate with your ex? Why?

12. What did you learn about yourself from your last relationship?

13. Was your ex-girlfriend/wife liked by your friends and family? Why or why not?

14. Have you ever been physically attracted to or had sex with a man?

15. Have you ever gotten a woman pregnant? What happened?

Maybe this list is not extensive enough. That's why I put in parentheses after the title to never stop asking questions.

Other questions to ask:

Are you saved? If so, how long have you been saved and what do you actually believe? If he/she is not saved, RUN!!!!

How often do you attend church?

What service(s) do you perform in your church? What ministry are you involved in?

What were your parents like? What was the greatest deed you ever did for your mother and father to show appreciation?

What is your relationship like with your children's mother and her family?

Do you have a bank account? Life insurance? Health insurance? Do you visit a doctor regularly and take good care of your body, mind, and soul?

What mutual funds do you own? How much stock have your purchased in the last year? What are your plans for retirement?

Have you ever had any repossessions? What is your credit score? (all of this reflects on you, if you join in marriage).

A declaration to myself...

I Forgive you

1. I forgive you for attempting to ruin my life: you had no hopes for your future, so you spent time trying to pull me down.

2. I forgive you for hitting me over and over again: you were not in control of your anger from your past and I was the closet person to you.

3. I forgive you for cursing me: you have no respect for your own character because you tried to control my destiny.

4. I forgive your accusations: you have so many skeletons and lack of repentance from your past you believe my life was and still is filled with promiscuity.

5. I forgive you for your lack of protection: you didn't know what your requirements are for being a Godly husband, even though the Word of God tells you everything.

6. I forgive you for not being a provider: you were so busy watching me work and prosper that you lost perspective on what true abundance was about...Trusting God becoming one together!

7. I forgive you for the disloyalty: you don't know what true loyalty is because you sold your soul to the enemy

to get to the top...which is not in your grasp, you're climbing someone else's ladder.

8. I forgive you for turning your children against me: you were not proud of your childhood and you do not want the best for your children.

9. I forgive you for disrespecting me: when you do not respect yourself, there are no guidelines for respecting others.

10. I forgive you for breaking my heart: considering your history, it's all you care to do.

11. I forgive you for disparaging my name: you have no idea that my name was established before I knew you and your attempts were wasted energy.

12. I forgive you for trying to place guilt upon me: my relationship with Christ freed me from the guilt of my past and I wanted to keep our lives blameless in the site of man.

13. I forgive you for cheating: you were never satisfied in relationships with your family and previous marriages, so you felt at ease to do what you do best.

14. I forgive you for lying to me and about me: when I understand who your true father is (satan-father of lies), I know why you feel like lying is good.

15. I forgive you for stealing my money, my time, my body: you were on assignment to kill, steal and destroy

any and everything I had to enjoy life, you didn't give it and you can't handle how God chooses to use it.

16. I forgive you for robbing me of life: you chose to live in bondage and you felt the need to drag me with you.

17. I forgive you for not praying for and with me: you're afraid of God doing great things in your life, but it takes FAITH...you lack it

18. I forgive you for not loving me with everything: you cannot give what you refuse to have...you believe marriage is 50/50.

19. I forgive you for thinking so lowly of me: you can only think of others as you truly think of yourself and God.

20. I forgive you for not accepting my family: you refuse to trust God's family, so I guess it's your job to choose your family 🤭

21. I forgive you for not paying bills: you had no established guidelines in your life to sustain the labor you put in, but not being able to hold a job doesn't help pay bills.

22. I forgive you for leaving me: when you're not use to good things, you never appreciate them; just as you stated to me, "You're too good to be true."

23. I forgive you for trying to keep me up at night: arguing and attempting to keep me tired and possibly

have an accident in route to work...God was always protecting me.

24. I forgive you for pushing me down: I never mind helping you up when needed...but I never expected you to kick me down once you got up.

25. I forgive you for not keeping your word: it's easy to say what you want rather than do it.

26. I forgive you for the wounds, broken heart, and shattered dreams: you said you never saw vision for our marriage, so why should I expect a great future with you?

Most of all...**I forgive me** for staying in something that God never meant for me to be in. I was not your rib, bone of your bone, flesh of your flesh. I was just a rejected transplant that you knew would never be a match. But thank God, He kept me, protected me, and helped me stay focused on Him.

I'm better

I'm stronger

I'm wiser

I'm healed and whole

I'm healthy and prosperous

Prayers that help me heal...

Prayer to stop divorce and restore marriage

Lord, I offer up my marriage to you, so that you may heal our wounds, and restore our union. Lord, I ask you to command my marriage to raise from the dead. I pray that you remove all evil influences and enemies of my marriage.

Speak to my husband, soften his heart, and return him to our marriage. I ask that you show my husband that our love is true and that together with God we can be happy again. Lord, you are a tremedous and loving God, and have the power to help spouses reconcile. Lord I ask that you "fix" me and my husband so that we will once again fall into love. Father, I ask that you help me remain calm during this difficult time, so that I may choose my words and actions carefully.

I pray that You speak to my husband in his thoughts, dreams, and visions. Show him that divorce is not the solution and will not make him happier. Only through our faith in You and our love in each other will we reach true happiness. Thank You, Lord for recieving my prayer and showing my husband the way home. AMEN.

Just in case, your marriage is not restored...in my case...BUT I was made whole and healed. I have learned to be content in whatever state that I am in...only God can bring you to a point of contentment, in the midst of pain and brokenness.

Lord, let Your will be done. In Jesus name, AMEN

My prayer to God:

Father, thank You for loving me just as I am. You are my husbandman and you have given me everything I need to function each day, moment by moment. You are my Provider, my Priest and Prophet, my Protector and Physician. I thank you for being the Giver of life and allowing me to live it abundantly. When so much is going on in my life, you have been the Sustainer and Maintainer of my soul, body, and spirit. You have been the Lord of my life.

Thank You, Lord for your provisions to make it as a wife abused, misused, damaged and shattered. You have allowed me to go through so much, not to destroy me, but to strengthen me and help me see that You are faithful, just, and true to Your promises.

Thank You for showing me who I was and who I am, as well as showing me what true LOVE really is. I thank You that LOVE is kind and suffers long; LOVE does not envy; LOVE does not parade itself; and is not puffed up; LOVE does not behave rudely, nor does it seek its own. LOVE is not provoked and thinks no evil. LOVE does not rejoice in iniquity but rejoices in the truth; LOVE bears all things, believes all things, hopes all things, endures all things. LOVE never fails. Where I failed to show

LOVE, I failed to display You. I ask for forgiveness and help me to always have the mind of Christ, especially during adversity.

I pray for comfort in my life. Lord, whether I find true love here on earth or I continue to allow You to console me every night, I look forward to whatever You have in store for me.

As I focus on You daily, please help me to have

- the innocence of Eve
- the leadership of Deborah
- the loyalty of Esther
- the faithfulness of Ruth
- the submissiveness of Sarah
- the dedication of Hannah
- the gentleness of the Shunamite woman
- the entrepreneurship of the widow woman
- the courage of Leah
- the humility of Rachal
- the organization of the Virtuous Woman
- the favor of Mary
- the stewardship of Phoebe
- the work ethics of Martha
- the teaching of Lois and Eunice
- the courage of the woman with the issue
- the valor of the woman at the well

It takes all these traits and more to function according to Your design. I may not exhibit them all at once, but I know because of Who You are in me, I will be steadfast, unmovable, always abounding in Your works to prove that I am the woman You fearfully and wonderfully made to have abundant life. A life that includes having the right man that You desire for me to have as a fit. Somewhere, some man is missing a rib. Not a missing toe, not a missing backbone, not a missing hand, nor a head injury. You have ordained me to walk next to him and have a companion as stated in Ecclesiastes and Amos. I expect for him to have desires to be whole with You as Your will is done on earth through him, as it is in heaven.

So, I patiently wait and look forward to the man that You have ordained for me to spend the rest of my life with. You have allowed me to enjoy some moments. I realize that there is nothing too hard for You. So, I thank you in advance for the right man and the best man that You provide. Help me to recognize what You have for me. Please do not allow me to go through any more years of playing house or wasting time with someone who does not have the value of marriage, which should represent Christ's return for His bride. Clean me! Purge me! Renew the right Spirit within me! Help me to be prepared for the king that You send to walk alongside me and understand how valuable I am to You and what a blessing I can be to him.

I trust You with my whole heart so that you can place it in the right life to be protected, provided for, and prayed over daily. I decree and declare that I will not suffer any more damage, brokenness, abuse, misuse, or manipulation due to incorrect decision making. I am sober, and I know You will allow only good to come to me. There is no good thing or man that You will withhold from me because of my faithfulness and obedience.

I will always seek You first and trust that You will add whatever I need, as well as desire.

Thank You in advance for answering my prayer and keeping me safe from the enemy. In Jesus' name, I believe and expect You to take care of Your daughter. Amen.

About the Author

Born in New Orleans, La, the 4th angel after 3 rugged boys to my parents Ernest and Gussie Bates. Raised in Mississippi in an extended family, which included my parents, grandparents, brothers and two cousins.

Graduate of the University of Kentucky with nursing Degree. Continued education at McKendree College with Bachelor of Science Degree in Nursing out of Chicago, Ill. Completed hours with Master's in Business Administration and towards Master's in Nursing from University of Phoenix. Completed requirements for Master's Degree in Christian Counseling from The Institute for Teaching God's Word in conjunction with American Academy of Christian Counseling. Earned a Doctor of Liberal Arts in Faith Based Crisis Counseling in June of 2016 and Doctor of Theology in 2017. This all led to the licensure and ordination for Crisis Counseling and ministry with more than 270 hours of continued education in helping those in the storm of abuse.

Veteran of the Air Force for 11 years, serving as a flight nurse in Operation Enduring Freedom out of Afghanistan during 911 conflict.

Spent many years in the diagnostic arena of medicine helping to develop and educate on lab tests that identify disease early, which leads to faster treatment and improved patient outcomes. Currently working as the Clinical Manager for a large cardiology clinic in Texas, leading a new generation of nurses and medical staff to improved, quality care using the I-CARE principles.

CEO/Founder of Draped in Praise Publishing that offers services to people looking to write and publish their works to improve the lives of others. Author of <u>The Woman at the Well: From Guilt to Grace</u> and <u>Damaged Goods: From Shattered Pieces to Sacred Peace</u>. My God-given vision includes opening a one-stop clinic to encompass healing in every aspect of life -physical, mental, emotional, spiritual and social for low-income, no-insurance, and low-educated people. I would love to bring back house calls for medical care and group therapy based on the Word of God and therapeutic healing.

A member of New Jerusalem Interdenominational Church in Rockdale TX under the covering of Dr. Dennis and Dr. Clara Brooks – Pastor, Professor, Prophet, Priest, Protector – who have helped to groom me for Godly success with the encouragement of my son, RJ (Robert Jr – scholar, Physical Therapy, soccer extraordinaire).

A Christian first with roles of wife, mother, nurse, consultant, dancer, cook, sports enthusiast, counselor, educator, prayer warrior and worshipper. ☺

Favorite Scriptures: Jeremiah 29:11, Ephesians 3:20, Matthew 6:33, and Psalm 16:3

www.ingramcontent.com/pod-product-compliance
Lightning Source LLC
Chambersburg PA
CBHW031601110426
42742CB00036B/645